JIM GRANT

UNICEF Visionary

This book has been written by former colleagues and friends of Jim Grant, with help and contributions from many others. We are grateful to the James P. Grant Trust for financial support for the editing and layout. We would also like to thank Bernadette Abegglen and Eve Leckey of the UNICEF Innocenti Research Centre in Florence for help with the printing and distribution of the book. In New York, we thank Ellen Tolmie and the UNICEF photo library for identifying and making available photographs. We thank Mary Cahill for her help in assembling a list of Jim Grant's contacts.

We express especial thanks to Ellan Young Grant for allowing us to use her own photographs of Jim taken during their travels together to see UNICEF programmes in different countries of the world.

We are also grateful for support from UNICEF, its field offices and national committees for help with the distribution and sales of the book.

Contact point:
UNICEF Innocenti Research Centre
Piazza Santissima Annunziata 12
50122 Florence, Italy

ISBN: 92-806-3723-1

Cover design: Rod Craig, MCC
Cover photograph: Joe Rubino

Text layout: Charlie Webster, Production Line
Photo credits: David Barbour, pages 18, 146; Dennis Budd Gray, page 37; John Isaac, pages 44, 158; Carlton James, page 145; Ruby Mera, page 136; Shehzad Noorani, page 110; Giacomo Pirozzi, page 66; Betty Press, page 88; Ellan Young, pages 17, 87, 157.

Printed on recycled paper by Tipografia Giuntina, Florence, Italy

Jim Grant (1922-1995)

Jim Grant was a remarkable man of truly worldwide influence. Born in China, he dedicated his whole life to the cause of international development: in USAID; as founder, President and Executive Director of the Overseas Development Council in Washington; and for his last 15 years, as Executive Director of UNICEF. He was a professional and a visionary, an analyst with vast experience and an activist of almost unlimited commitment. But it was during his time as head of UNICEF that his vision, skills and leadership came together to make a worldwide impact. At the time of his death it was estimated that, because of his influence, at least 25 million children were alive who would otherwise have died in early life.

This book gives glimpses of his leadership and achievements during his period as Executive Director of UNICEF. Each piece is written by one of his close colleagues – one of those who was privileged to share in the heady excitement of the efforts and victories for children during those intense years. Many others could have contributed to this volume. For Jim was an inclusive leader, always reaching out to mobilize everyone for children and readily acknowledging the contributions of others, inside UNICEF and the UN and far beyond. We hope this helps to rekindle his vision and carry on his global mission for children.

R.J.

About the contributors

Carol Bellamy has been Executive Director of UNICEF since 1995.

Peter Adamson was for fifteen years the author of UNICEF's annual *State of the World's Children Report*. Before this, he was founder-editor of *The New Internationalist* magazine and a writer and presenter of BBC television documentaries on development issues. He has also published two novels, including one set in the developing world.

Sheila Barry Tacon was a UNICEF staff-member from 1975 to 1994. Over this period, she was Assistant Secretary of the Executive Board, Chief of the Non-Governmental Affairs Office in New York, Women and Child Survival Officer in Nairobi, and finally UNICEF Representative in Botswana. Since 1995, she has been closely involved with the UNICEF history programme.

Kul Gautam is Deputy Executive Director (Alliances and Resources) for UNICEF, a position he has held since 2000. Before this, he was for three years Regional Director of UNICEF for South East Asia and the Pacific and from 1993 Director of Programme Division in New York. Over his career, he has worked for UNICEF in a variety of positions from programme officer to UNICEF representative in Laos, Haiti and India. He was the key UNICEF staff member responsible for preparing the draft Declaration and Plan of Action for the World Summit for Children in 1990.

Richard Jolly, a development economist, worked with Jim Grant as UNICEF's Deputy Executive Director (Programmes) from 1982 to 1995. Before this he was Director of the Institute of Development Studies at the University of Sussex, where he is currently an Honorary Professor and Research Associate. From 1996 to 2000 he was special Coordinator of UNDP's Human Development Report.

Nyi Nyi was invited by Jim Grant in 1980 to become Director of Programme Development and Planning Division. Later he was appointed Director of UNICEF's Programme Division, where he provided global oversight of the programmes for Child Survival and Development and Universal Child Immunisation. From 1990 to1995, he provided support for follow up to the mid-decade goals of the World Summit for Children. Before joining UNICEF, he was deputy Minister of Education in Burma where he master-minded the literacy campaign. Since retiring from UNICEF, he has been Clinical Professor in public health at Tulane University and a member of the technical expert committee of the International Trachoma Initiative.

Mary Racelis, a sociologist from the Philippines, was UNICEF's Senior Policy Adviser on Family and Child Welfare from 1979-83. In this capacity, she was also responsible for programme issues relating to women and community participation and from1981-83 she served also as Chairperson of the Global Staff Association. From 1983 until her retirement in 1992, she was UNICEF Regional Director for Eastern and Southern Africa, based in Nairobi, Kenya.

Richard Reid joined UNICEF from Save the Children in 1980. He served there-after as Representative in Nigeria; Representative in Turkey; Regional Director for the Middle East and North Africa; Director of Public Affairs; and regional head of the Former Socialist Countries until retirement in 1995. Earlier he was a Peace Corps country director, and head-master at Robert College in Istanbul, where he now teaches international relations at Bilgi University.

Jon Rohde, a doctor and public health specialist, was a key adviser to Jim Grant on Child Survival and Development from 1980 to 1995 and, from 1990 to 1997, UNICEF's Representative in India. Before this, he had worked in Indonesia for Rockefeller Foundation, in Bangladesh on cholera research and in Haiti as a Director with Management Sciences for Health (MSH). Since leaving UNICEF, he has directed the MSH EQUITY Project restructuring health services in South Africa.

Contents

Foreword by President Jimmy Carter

Jim Grant

It was one of my privileges as President to suggest to the United Nations Secretary General the names of very senior Americans who could play leadership roles within the UN. I am proud to acknowledge that I nominated Jim Grant to the post of Executive Director of UNICEF, and I was pleased when the Secretary General appointed Jim to the post.

Jim Grant brought vision, commitment and extraordinary leadership skills to UNICEF, a unique organization which always has had a special place in the hearts of Americans as well as in the hearts and lives of millions of people from other countries around the world.

I followed UNICEF's progress under Jim Grant, especially the mobilizing efforts to achieve a child survival and development revolution in all regions of the world. I admired his skill in winning the interest and commitment of many national leaders to work toward these goals for the children in their own countries. I was pleased personally to support these efforts. I was delighted a few years later to join the celebration and formal certification ceremony marking the achievement of 80 percent coverage of immunization coverage of children in developing countries.

Our concerns for children in need, especially in conflict situations, have taken Rosalynn and me to all continents many times over the years to encourage the actions needed to ensure this general victory also is achieved for children living in war-torn areas, such as Sudan. Polio and Guinea worm can never be eradicated from the face of the earth – and thus for future generations – unless they are totally eliminated in the most difficult places.

Jim Grant and UNICEF colleagues in all parts of the world have demonstrated how the organizations of the UN can provide international leadership to fulfill the rights and needs of children everywhere, rich and poor. I hope this book of first-hand experiences of Jim Grant's leadership and vision will help rekindle the spirit and commitment of many others to follow in the path he charted forward.

President Jimmy Carter presents an award to Jim Grant, Atlanta, 1989.

A tribute

My predecessors as Executive Director of the United Nations Children's Fund – Maurice Pate, Henry Labouisse and James P. Grant – were all leaders of extraordinary dedication and commitment to the cause of children. It is because of their efforts that UNICEF is the foremost advocate for children the world over – a distinction given triumphal recognition in 1965, when the agency was awarded the Nobel Peace Prize for its work; and again in 1990, when world leaders gathered in unprecedented numbers to affirm a visionary agenda at the World Summit for Children.

Jim Grant, a man of prodigious energies and missionary zeal, came to UNICEF at a time when the challenges seemed more daunting than ever. It was a time when 15 million young children were dying every year of readily preventable causes; when 300 million children were malnourished; when a billion people, half of them children, lacked access to safe water, and when a quarter of the world's children never saw the inside of a classroom, and half never finished elementary school.

The staggering scale and utter needlessness of these numbers made a deep impression on Jim, and he had no qualms in describing the situation for what it was: a scandal. Incremental progress was no longer acceptable. What was needed, he realized, was a quantum leap – the launch of nothing less than a revolution in child survival and development, based on the principle that the well-being of children, starting with dramatic gains in the survival rates of the youngest, is a basic precondition of healthy development.

Jim Grant dedicated his life to that revolution. During his 15 year tenure as Executive Director, the number of countries where UNICEF worked doubled, the size of UNICEF's field staff tripled, and its income quadrupled. He saw to it that UNICEF-assisted programmes in developing countries functioned as demonstration projects that others could emulate and take to scale. But Jim also understood that the revolution's success hinged on the creation of a global constituency for children and that, to build that constituency, UNICEF had to hone its salesmanship in the marketplace of ideas, showing why realigning public policies and resources in favour of children is the key to a just and peaceful world.

Working through the UN System and the international development community, he earned a reputation for setting goals that more timid souls saw as overly ambitious – like universal child immunization – while relentlessly building the support needed to achieve them. And therein lay the secret of Jim's success: his understanding that the very boldness of UNICEF's goals for children would help stir the political impetus necessary to achieve them.

Using the same visionary approach, Jim expedited the adoption of the Magna Carta for child rights – the 1989 Convention on the Rights of the Child. By putting UNICEF's institutional weight behind the treaty's ratification, Jim helped set in motion a process that not only brought the Convention into force faster than any other human rights instrument then or since but ultimately made it the most widely embraced rights treaty in history. The 1990 World Summit for Children, the largest gathering of world leaders in history until that time, was the culmination of Jim's vision to mobilize the world's leadership for children.

Jim Grant – UNICEF Visionary is a testament to the vision and accomplishments of a giant of a man whose legacy continues to inspire us all in UNICEF and beyond. Written by colleagues who worked closely with Jim, it chronicles actions and initiatives that originated under his leadership and that continue to protect the lives and well-being of countless millions of children around the world. As we prepare for a United Nations General Assembly Special Session on Children in September 2001, and the launch of a global movement for children, the lessons of Jim Grant's leadership as documented in this book will be a tremendous source of inspiration to us all.

CAROL BELLAMY
Executive Director, UNICEF

With the President of Bolivia during the 1997 salt iodization campaign.

The mad American

Peter Adamson

This essay was originally presented as a UNICEF lecture at the Church House Conference Centre, London, June 16, 1997

The title of this story is 'The mad American'. And its central character is James Pineo Grant.

At the time the story opens, Jim Grant is 57 years old and already has a distinguished – apparently conventional – career behind him: Deputy Director of the United States aid programme; head of various US aid missions; President of a prestigious Washington think-tank; Trustee of the Rockefeller Foundation.

But our story opens in 1979, when President Carter nominates Jim Grant to become the new head of UNICEF.

UNICEF needs little introduction here. Headquarters in New York. Offices in nearly every country. Several thousand employees. National committees in many industrialized countries. Running programmes to help children throughout the developing world.

Changing gears

The 1980s open and the new head of UNICEF moves into his New York office overlooking the East River. He begins conventionally enough. Travelling. Listening. Learning about the organization.

The first sign that something different is about to happen comes at a place called Sterling Forest. It's a rather plush, corporate conference centre about two hours north of New York City. Not really UNICEF's style. Jim Grant has invited maybe a hundred people. Mostly UNICEF staff from around the world. A few outsiders. The idea is to discuss UNICEF's future – and for the new Executive Director to outline his own thinking on the subject.

Well, over the three days of the meeting, Jim Grant does outline his thinking. But he succeeds mainly in mystifying and alarming people. The phrase he uses again and again is that he wants UNICEF to shift gears. He feels the organization has been going along nicely in second. Now he wants to see a rapid shift to third, and then fourth.

People exchange glances across the room.

He isn't interested, he says, in incremental increase. He doesn't want to know about a five per cent or ten per cent a year improvement in UNICEF's performance. What he wants is a quantum leap. He wants UNICEF's impact on the world to increase ten-fold, fifty-fold, a hundred-fold. And he wants it to happen quickly.

Smiles are still being exchanged across the room. But the smiles are growing distinctly more nervous.

So how do we make this quantum leap, he asks. How do we shift gears? How do we punch above our weight? How do we get more bang for our buck? We have a few hundred million dollars, he says. That's three or four cents for every child in the developing countries. We can't change the world with that. In any case, what changes the world isn't budgets and projects and programmes. What changes the world, is a major shift in thinking, brought about by advocacy, new ideas, new visions. Putting all this together, and ever one to mix a metaphor if he possibly could, the new Executive Director says that UNICEF's main objective under his leadership will be leverage in the market place of ideas.

In the days and weeks that followed Sterling Forest, alarm bells rang out in UNICEF offices across the world. Shifting gears. Quantum leaps. Advocacy. Changing the world. Leverage. Market place of ideas. Had anyone told him that this was UNICEF?

And as always on such occasions, an informal consensus rapidly developed in the bars and the corridors and the coffee lounges. And the word at Sterling Forest was – 'American'. He's very 'American'.

The big idea

Within months, the big idea that Jim Grant is looking for – the idea that would allow UNICEF to multiply its impact in the world – is almost handed to him on a plate.

Or rather in a paper – a paper given at an academic conference in Birmingham, England, by a Dr. Jon Eliot Rohde.

I can't do justice to that extraordinary lecture here. But let me try to sum up in a sentence what it was about it that changed the course of UNICEF for the next 15 years. It was the proposition that more than half of all the death and disease among the children of the developing world was simply unnecessary – because it was now relatively easily and cheaply preventable.

Let me also try to telescope into a couple of paragraphs the argument behind this contention.

About 14 million young children were dying in the developing world every year. And the great majority of this death and disease could be laid at the door of just five or six common illnesses – measles, tetanus, whooping cough, pneumonia, diarrhoeal disease – often in conjunction with poor nutrition. These were the same diseases that had taken a similar toll in Europe and North America right up until the early part of this century. The difference was that there were now low-cost means of prevention or cure for almost all of them.

Vaccines had long been available to protect children against measles, tetanus, whooping cough and polio. There had been recent technological advances in such areas as heat-stability, and the costs had fallen dramatically. Yet only about 15 per cent of children in the poor world were being immunized. And these diseases were still killing four or five million children every year. Similarly, trials had proved that cheap oral rehydration therapy (ORT) could prevent most of the dehydration, caused by diarrhoeal disease, that was killing over three million children every year.

And it wasn't just a question of saving lives – the sheer frequency of all these common illnesses saps the mental development and physical growth of even larger numbers of survivors.

And it was now so *unnecessary*. The methods of prevention or treatment were tried and tested, available and affordable. But they had not been put at the disposal of those who needed them. The bridge had not been built between what science knows and what people needed.

This analysis obviously drew on a large body of work in child health by people like David Morley, then Professor of Child Health at London University, who had devoted much of his life to precisely this cause of developing and promoting low cost methods of protecting children's lives and health.

After reading the Birmingham lecture, Jim Grant spent some time travelling with Jon Rohde in China and in Haiti, being shown in flesh and blood what the lecture had shown in facts and figures. And when he got back to New York he knew that he had found his big idea. He knew how UNICEF was going to change gears and multiply its impact in the world.

A child survival revolution

September 1982. Jim Grant calls another meeting. A more modest affair. UNICEF headquarters in New York. A weekend. About 20 people. Senior UNICEF staff. Some outsiders. The purpose is, once again, to brain-storm on UNICEF's future role and direction.

But if what came out of the Sterling Forest meeting was alarmingly vague, what came out of the New York meeting was quite terrifyingly specific.

Gradually, Jim worked the meeting round to his big proposal. He wanted UNICEF to launch a worldwide child survival revolution. He wanted UNICEF to lead a campaign to halve child deaths across the developing world. He wanted UNICEF to set itself the aim of cutting the toll of disease and disability on an unprecedented scale. And he wanted to do it by means of a massive, focused effort to make three or four low cost techniques like immunization and ORT available to almost every child in every developing country.

The audacity of this proposition is almost impossible now to recapture. At that time, UNICEF projects – anybody's projects – in the developing world were reaching out to a few hundred, very occasionally thousands, of children in villages here and neighbourhoods there. Now Jim Grant was talking about reaching out to four or five hundred million children in the developing world, and to the 100 million that were being born into it each year.

To begin with, he said that immunization levels had to be doubled – to 40 per cent by the mid-1980s. And then doubled again – to 80 per cent by the end of the 1980s.

Then there was ORT – the salts and water solution that can prevent death from diarrhoeal disease. At the time, the technique was virtually unknown.

Jim said it must be put at the disposal of at least half the families in the developing world within a few years.

ORT and immunization weren't the only priorities. But they were what Jim liked to call the twin engines of a child survival revolution.

These were simply staggering proposals. And it is impossible now, all these years later, to recapture the full sense of how extraordinary they seemed at the time. I couldn't tell you how many times I heard the phrase *'he's mad'* in the days and weeks that followed.

The tanker and the speedboat

I too had read Jon Rohde's original lecture. And I had devoted a good deal of the draft *State of the World's Children* report for that year to what I thought was rather a passionate advocacy of its prescriptions. But it was a handwringing piece. It was a 'something ought to be done' piece. And it wasn't enough. Jim wanted the report – about to go out in dozens of languages to every newspaper and magazine and every radio and television station in every country – to announce and launch his Child Survival Revolution.

The Director of Information for UNICEF at that time was my good friend and colleague John Williams. He and I pleaded with Jim to think again. To consult more widely. To let people in the organization have their say. To take just a few more months. To refine the idea before launching it into the world.

Jim would have none of it. I remember arguing with him late one night and saying to him *'this organization is a 200,000 tonne vessel with a fifteen mile turning circle – it's an oil tanker and you're trying to drive it like a speedboat.'* I knew straightaway that it was entirely the wrong thing to say. His eyes lit up as he saw himself at the helm of a oil tanker, throwing the throttle, changing up a gear, watching the prow rise up in the water, taking off across the high seas.

He went ahead with the announcement of the Child Survival Revolution. And again it is almost impossible, now, to recapture the reaction. But at the time you could see the shock on people's faces. You could feel it in the canteens and the corridors. Attempting anything on this scale was clearly mad. UNICEF would fall flat on its face. UNICEF couldn't do it. Nobody could do it. The money wasn't there. The roads and the transport systems weren't there. The clinics, the vaccinators, the electricity supply, the fridges, the cold chains, the communications capacity – even the demand wasn't there. None of it was in place for action on this scale.

And even if it were, could UNICEF really start focusing everything on immunization and ORT? What about education, water supply, sanitation, housing, street children? It seemed to be throwing out all UNICEF's history and priorities – throwing away years of commitment to integrated development strategies, basic services, and people's participation. It was reducing the prized complexities of development to the contents of a sachet and a syringe. It was top-down. It was technological fix. It was tunnel visioned. It was, as the World Health Organization said, monofocal.

The reaction, in short, was overwhelmingly negative – inside UNICEF itself, inside the other UN agencies, in government circles, among development professionals and academics.

Turmoil

Some opposed Jim Grant out of fear of upheaval and failure; out of innate conservatism; out of not wanting comfortable routines to be disturbed. Others had more legitimate concerns about the whole approach. There was hardly anyone involved at the time who did not have the most serious doubts about what Jim Grant was proposing. And this story would be romanticized, untruthful, if I did not try to capture some of the turmoil of that time. I myself was certainly sceptical. And my worries were perhaps not untypical.

Anyone who has worked in this field knows that development is the most subtle and complex of processes; knows that the answers are not primarily technological but political and social; knows, too, that there are great dangers to imposing simplified strategies from the outside. Also, at a time when so many of the world's poor were becoming poorer – as debt mounted, commodity prices fell, and aid declined – it did not seem right to be going into battle for vaccinations and oral rehydration salts alone. It felt like relinquishing the real struggle.

And, speaking for myself, I dislike and distrust simplicities and certainties, and sound-bites and single-mindedness. They are the close cousins of intolerance and imposition.

And yet...

There is a danger that complexity can itself be a kind of comfort, an excuse for inaction, a kind of liberal paralysis. And many of us, I remember, were tired and frustrated with campaigning on a broad front and seeming to get nowhere. And who could not be struck by the sheer unforgiveableness of millions upon millions of children dying and having their normal development undermined – when the means to prevent it were at hand? It was as if a cheap cure for cancer had been discovered but no-one had bothered making it available. And if that comparison sounds far fetched, it is only because we are hearing it from the perspective of a rich society. If you look at the figures, the analogy is fairly exact.

And hanging over all this turmoil and doubt, was the sheer and obvious impossibility of UNICEF attempting anything on this scale.

Well ... these were some of the considerations.

But for me the decisive factor was probably something more trivial. I have always loved words and the English language. And if Jim Grant's enemies were going to accuse him of 'monofocality' then I was always going to be on his side.

So Lesley and I and many others decided that we would go with the mad idea, that we would help Jim Grant to run this one up the flagpole. I was becoming more American every day.

The dark days

The early days were pretty dark. There were many inside and outside the organization who were scathing and hostile. So much so that at this time Jim's position was in some danger. There was talk of getting rid of him. There were murmurs of mutiny in the ranks. There were rumours that his contract would not be renewed – the equivalent of the governments of the world firing Jim Grant as head of UNICEF.

And the organization itself came round behind him only slowly. It turned out to be an oil tanker after all. But turn it did.

The Executive Director has power to hire and fire, power to promote or pass over, power to include or exclude from inner counsels. These are the crude instruments of internal direction changing in any large organization. And Jim used them.

But many more came around for better reasons. There was the faultless public health logic of the case for making this attempt. And there was the personality of the man himself. The idealism and commitment were so obviously genuine – in all those years I never heard anyone question this. For all the grand plans, Jim Grant personally was devoid of self-importance. And for all the high profile campaigning that was to come, he never sought the spotlight for himself. For Jim, it was only and always the cause. And I believe that in the end it was this as much as anything else that won so many to his side.

And so, in the early and mid-1980s, work began on the grand plan.

Going to scale

The problem was essentially one of scale. The world that Jim Grant came into, as the new head of a UN agency, was by and large a world of small-scale projects, of pilot studies, field trials, research and demonstration programmes. And the question he made everyone confront was – how do you go to scale? How do you take known solutions and put them into action on the same scale as the problems?

Now of course you can't even think about reaching out to people on this scale without governments. And that means you have to have political will. If only the political leaderships of nations were committed, then of course these things could be attempted across whole countries – with aid from the international community and help from UNICEF and others.

Political will. How many late night conversations have ended with the words *'you can't do anything without political will.'* How many plans and potentials have come to nothing for the lack of this political will?

Jim Grant's response was: *'Well, we'll just have to create the political will.'*

Creating the will

He began an astonishing odyssey. Over the next few years, he travelled many hundreds of thousands of miles and met with the great majority of political leaders in the developing world. I am confident in saying that no one has ever held one-to-one discussions with anything like as many of the world's presidents and prime ministers as Jim Grant did in those years.

And these were not ceremonial meetings or photo opportunities. He cut through all of that and made his pitch. He was never without his sachet of oral rehydration salts. And he was never without the key statistics for that country. He would ask every president and prime minister he met if he or she knew what the country's immunization rate was, and how many of the country's children were being killed and disabled by vaccine-preventable disease or dehydration, and how little it would cost to prevent it.

To see him in action in these meetings was truly astonishing. He would tell heads of state that other countries were doing much better, or that their neighbours were racing ahead, or that he needed some far-sighted political leader to set an example to the whole world of what could be done. He would point out to a president that economically his or her country was ten times more developed than, say, Sri Lanka, but had a far lower immunization rate and a far higher child death rate. He would point out that the protection being given to children was lagging well behind what could be expected for a nation of this standing.

He didn't complicate matters with other issues. For heads of state, he said, you have to pitch in with a simple, doable proposition. You appeal to their idealism, but you also tell them how they can drastically reduce child deaths at a cost they can afford and on a time scale that can bring them political dividends.

He cajoled and persuaded and flattered and shamed and praised. He offered aid money that he didn't have, and he offered help that the UNICEF country office often wasn't in a position to give. And he back-slapped and shook hands with them all, whether democratic leaders or dire dictators. He shook hands that were stained with blood, hands that had turned the keys on political prisoners, hands that had signed away human rights, hands that were deep in the country's till.

Some of this I was occasionally unhappy about, as were others. We worried about the lending of UNICEF's good name to corrupt and inhuman regimes. But Jim's answer was always the same. *We don't like the President so the kids don't get immunized?' 'You want to wait to launch the campaign until all governments are respectable?'*

And he was shameless in other ways too. There were so many examples, but I have time only for one. Sometime in the late 1980s Jim had had some peel-off stickers made – printed with the words 'Child Survival Revolution'. We had been in the Dominican Republic to see the President. And the President was so taken with Jim that he gave a grand dinner in his honour. There was the President, wearing a million dollar suit and flanked by three or four generals. The President asked Jim to make a speech. Half way through his pitch on what the President could do for the children of the Dominican Republic, Jim looked at the generals behind the President's chair. Pausing, he reached into his pocket.

'You know Mr. President,' he said, *'the Child Survival Revolution also needs its generals. And I want to create you a five star general of the Child Survival*

Revolution.' And he began putting little stickers all over the President's million dollar suit.

When we got back to our hotel, Jim's wife Ethel turned to him and said *'Jim, you are such a ham.'* Ham or not, I watched the President of the Dominican Republic on national television the next night and he was calling for the immunizing of all the nation's children and waving a little sachet of ORS at the camera.

Social mobilization

Jim's solution to the lack of resources and infrastructure for action on this scale was just as bold. Everywhere he went he called for 'social mobilization'.

The job called for a massive reaching out – not only to ensure supply but to create demand. And in most countries it clearly couldn't be handled by health services alone. Jim's answer was to enlist every possible outreach resource in the society – the teachers, the religious leaders, the media, the business community, the army, the police force, the non-governmental organizations, the youth movements, the women's organizations and the community groups. He appealed to them all to get involved.

The strain on UNICEF offices was something entirely new. Most responded magnificently. But performance now was measurable. There was a bottom line. What were the figures for immunization and ORT? And how fast were they rising?

There was no hiding place. And I think I can best illustrate this pressure by one other example. Jim was constantly asking for progress reports from UNICEF representatives in every country. And on one occasion he asked the UNICEF Representative for El Salvador why the immunization level there was failing to rise. The Representative replied that El Salvador was in the middle of a civil war and that most of the country was a no-go area. Most people would have thought that was a reasonable answer. Jim's reply – said straight out – was: *'Well, why don't they stop the war so they can immunize the kids?'*

It was just the kind of remark that made people think he was unbalanced.

In the following weeks, Jim Grant flew to El Salvador. He and the UNICEF staff in the country enlisted the help of the Catholic church and met with both government and the guerrilla leaders, and within a few months both sides in the civil war had agreed to call three separate days of cease-fire so that the nation's children could be immunized. And this happened ever year for several years until the war came to an end.

There were very few excuses that would satisfy Jim Grant for not reaching out to the children of the whole country. And a little thing like a civil war wasn't one of them.

In any situation where a job looked impossible, Jim's approach was always to look for leverage points. How can we 'end-run' this one was always his question. And again, I have time for only the briefest of examples. Soon after the assassination of Indira Gandhi, Jim flew to New Delhi. He saw the new Prime Minister, Rajiv Gandhi. And he proposed to him that the immunization of India's children should be the living memorial to his mother, Indira. Rajiv Gandhi agreed. And he had the monitoring of immunization levels put down as a regular item at cabinet meetings.

Promotion and criticism

These examples are only an indication of the colossal amount of work done in these years to create the political will and initiate action on a nation-wide scale in country after country. And backing all of this up was a major world-wide media campaign by UNICEF. A great many people were involved. Everybody in UNICEF had to become a promoter. And the annual *State of the World's Children* report and, later, *The Progress of Nations*, were only the flagships. But it was here the message was preached and the arguments made. Here the organization was primed and armed. Here the figures were set out, the critics answered, the successes and failures recorded. And it was all directed towards one end – helping to stimulate action on the necessary scale.

And the job was not only one of promotion. There was also a defence to be conducted. You can't expect to attempt something on this scale without critic-ism. The critics said that the whole effort would be self-defeating because it would only fuel population increase. They said that the children being saved by vaccines or ORT would only die of something else because UNICEF wasn't tackling the fundamental problems of poverty. They said that by concentrating only on saving lives UNICEF was ignoring the quality of life of the survivors.

None of these points is valid. But they are all superficially plausible. And they were battles that had to be fought, year after year, article after article, reply after reply.

And at this time, Jim's position – and the outcome of the colossal gamble he had taken – were still in doubt. The only thing that could save it all was results.

First results

By the middle of the 1980s, those results were beginning to come through.

Nations were beginning to make serious commitments. And immunization and ORT rates were beginning to rise. Overall, the proportion of the developing world's children who were immunized doubled to 40 per cent. And the use of life-saving ORT rose from almost nothing to the point where the therapy was being used by over a quarter of the families in the developing world.

Already, these were results on an entirely unprecedented scale.

Now change like this doesn't come about just because Jim Grant meets the president, or because the issues are put across to governments and the media. UNICEF people all over the world, and their counterparts in governments and in several other UN agencies worked to make it happen, to translate the political will into practical action on the ground. WHO, in particular, provided scientific advice on cold-chains and vaccine quality, and trained thousands of immunization managers. Hundreds of non-governmental organizations were becoming involved. Rotary International alone raised over $300 million dollars and mobilized its volunteers in a hundred countries. There are many thousands of actors in this story, and I'm very conscious of leaving so many of them out of this account.

But the point is that Jim Grant and UNICEF were supplying the one ingredient that had always been missing – the new sense of scale, the push for political will, the mobilization of so many other people and organizations in support of common, measurable goals.

And as the figures rose, support began to swing behind Jim Grant.

Everywhere UNICEF national committees, as well as fundraising and lobbying, made sure that governments took notice. And at a time when aid was falling and all other UN budgets were being cut back, UNICEF's budget was on its way to doubling to more than a billion dollars a year. The critics fell quiet. The noise of internal battle began to die down. And ORT and immunization rates continued to rise.

Iodine and vitamin A

But as the world moved towards the 1990s, the size of the task also began to increase.

For example, it was established beyond reasonable doubt that lack of vitamin A was responsible for approximately two million child deaths a year –

and for leaving at least a quarter of a million children permanently blinded each year. It was a tragedy that could be prevented by vitamin A capsules – at a cost of about two cents per child per year. By all the same reasoning that had taken UNICEF this far, this finding could not be ignored.

Similarly, it also became established that the biggest cause of preventable mental retardation among the world's children was lack of iodine in the diet. New studies showed that iodine deficiency – a very little known problem – was affecting 50 million children under five. It was causing 100,000 infants a year to be born as cretins. It was causing tens of millions of children to have lower IQs, so that they were not doing as well as they should in school. This tragedy, too, could be prevented – as it was in the industrialized nations – by iodizing all salt. The cost, in relation to the potential benefits, was negligible. And this, too, simply could not be ignored.

It is not just that these were important problems touching large numbers of children. There are plenty of important problems facing the world's children. The point is that these were problems for which solutions were available and affordable. So much so that it was unconscionable not to put them into action, not to do what it was now so obviously possible to do. Morality must march with capacity.

A World Summit for Children

I can't evade some small share of responsibility for the next mad idea.

To push for action on all of these fronts, Jim began looking for faster ways to create political will, to spell out to presidents and prime ministers – and the public – what could be done.

October 1988. We were flying back to New York. Jim began talking about organizing an international conference to try to get all these things moving at the same time. I told him the world was bored with UN conferences. They're seen as talk shops, with never any action afterwards. It would only be worth it if we could get, not delegates, but presidents and prime ministers to come together to talk about what could be done for children.

Well, the madder the idea, the more likely it was to appeal. And before we landed, Jim had decided to attempt a World Summit for Children.

Over the next eighteen months, he willed it into being. UNICEF could not convene a summit of world leaders. But in a few months, Jim persuaded the Prime Ministers of Canada, Sweden, and Pakistan, and the Presidents of

Mexico and Mali, to form a special committee to convene a World Summit. He persuaded Margaret Thatcher and George Bush to come. And soon, over 70 of the world's presidents and prime ministers had agreed to attend. It was to be the largest ever gathering of heads of state under one roof.

Then the idea ran into some problems. Protocol was being handled by an inter-governmental committee. They announced that all the heads of state would have to make a speech – all seventy-odd of them. So there would be no time for any other speakers. Not even Jim Grant. This defeated the whole point. We had thought they would be coming to listen to what could be done for children. We had forgotten Adlai Stevenson's warning that a politician is someone who approaches every question with an open mouth.

UNICEF protested. And after a struggle, Jim was allocated four minutes to address the assembled world leaders. We try to condense the message. But it cannot be done in four minutes. So we tell the committee it will be inter-minably boring; all those speeches one after another; there must surely be a video; all conferences have a video. They agree – maximum 12 minutes. They also agree that Jim's speech can follow directly after the film. We have 16 minutes to make the pitch.

I came back to London to see my friend and colleague Peter Firstbrook, a senior producer at the BBC. We had no time to shoot anything new. We began cutting and pasting past films that we had made together. The film was written as one presentation with Jim's speech. And it was screened to the assembled heads of state at the World Summit for Children. UNICEF also organized for it to be shown on national television stations in almost 90 countries on that same day. The film was called '341' – named after the number of children who will die unnecessarily during the 12 minutes the film takes to screen.

Target met

The World Summit for Children came together in late September 1990 – and UNICEF and WHO were able to make the big announcement. The target of 80 per cent immunization – the target that so many had said was impossible only a few years earlier – had been met across the developing world.

It was an absolutely vital announcement, not only for the millions of lives a year that immunization was now saving but for the credibility it lent to the proceedings, and to all the other targets now being proposed.

Everybody at UNICEF worked frantically behind the scenes. New goals to protect children, including goals for iodine and vitamin A, were agreed. And all of the heads of state present committed themselves to drawing up nation-wide plans.

Over the next five years the pressure on UNICEF, on headquarters, on the country offices, on the national committees, was intense – to raise more funds, to lift public support, to keep governments up to their promises, to maintain and increase immunization rates, to promote breastfeeding, to step up the pace on ORT and vitamin A, to make sure that all salt was iodized,

A scorecard

I cut rapidly now to 1995. And I want to give you a brief scorecard.

Almost all nations – one hundred and twenty nine in all – have by now reached, and sustained, immunization levels of 80 per cent or more. Compared with the toll in 1980, more than three million child deaths from measles, tetanus, and whooping cough are being prevented every year. And the normal growth of many millions more is being at least partially protected.

Meanwhile the number of children being crippled by polio has fallen from 400,000 a year in 1980 to under 100,000 a year in 1995. And as we sit here this evening, there are at least 3 million children in the developing world who are walking and running and playing normally who would be crippled for life by polio were it not for this extraordinary effort.

And what of the other main 'engines' of the child survival revolution?

ORT is being used in some form by about two thirds of all the families in the developing world – saving at least a million young lives a year.

Iodine deficiency, and the mass mental retardation it causes, is close to defeat. Of the more than 90 developing countries with iodine deficiency problems, 82 have now passed laws requiring the iodization of all salt – and most are close to the target of 90 per cent salt iodization. In total, 1.5 billion more people are consuming iodized salt today than in 1990. And at least 12 million children a year are being protected from some degree of mental damage.

Vitamin A promotion is moving more slowly. But it's moving. Seventeen developing nations, including some of the largest, have already eliminated vitamin A deficiency and the deaths and the blindness it was inflicting on their children. And 24 more countries have now launched nationwide programmes.

The end

These are only the highlights of what was achieved during those incredible years. And all Jim Grant could think about was how much more there was to do. He was then 72 years old and showing not the slightest sign of slowing down.

Then came the news that Jim Grant was in hospital. And soon everybody knew that Jim had cancer. Operations followed. And chemotherapy. And radiation.

Throughout, he refused to concede anything to his illness. He almost never referred to it. Once or twice I worked with him in the Sloane Kettering cancer hospital in New York as he waited to go in for his next session. His concentration on what we were doing was total.

And he refused to slow down.

In the last year of his life, when he was visibly ill and failing in body, he travelled tens of thousands of miles and held meetings with over 40 presidents and prime ministers, building the political will to achieve the new goals that had been set at the World Summit for Children. He still carried his ORS sachet. He still berated world leaders with figures and comparisons.

And he was still shameless. He now also carried in his pocket a small dropper of liquid. Dropped onto salt, the liquid turned blue if the salt had been iodized. And at state banquets in capital cities across the developing world, Jim would wait for an appropriate moment and then ask the president or prime minister to please pass the salt.

Jim Grant died in a small hospital in upstate New York in February 1995.

The last few hours of his life were immensely moving. It sounds like an over-dramatic figure of speech to say that someone fights for a cause until the last breath in his body. In Jim Grant's case, it was quite literally true. In the last hours of that last morning in the hospital, as he drifted in and out of consciousness, he was still struggling to map out the strategy for the next Executive Board meeting of UNICEF.

But for Jim the battle was at an end. All around him in the hospital room were letters and cards from virtually every country in the world, including from many of the presidents and prime ministers he had pushed and persuaded so hard.

On the cupboard by his bedside was a card from President Clinton. It said: *'I am writing to thank you from the bottom of my heart for your service to*

America, to UNICEF, and most of all to the children of the world.'

A few days later, a memorial service for Jim Grant was held at the Cathedral of St John the Divine on New York's upper West Side. It is the largest cathedral in the world. And it was full to overflowing with more than 3,000 people who had come to pay tribute to the 'Mad American'. They included Hilary Clinton and several members of the Clinton cabinet who had flown in from Washington for the service.

I can't list all of the hundreds of tributes here. Chinese Premier Li Peng wrote that Jim's death was *'an irretrievable loss to the children of the world.'* Nelson Mandela wrote to say that *'his death is a great loss to each and every needy child in this world.'* Former President Jimmy Carter said that his nomination of Jim Grant to head UNICEF was one of the greatest and most lasting achievements of his Presidency. And the New York Times, the paper that Jim had loved, mourned the passing of *'one of the great Americans of this century.'*

A place to stand

I have only been able to give the edited highlights of this story. And I have not told of some of the set-backs and disappointments, failures and mistakes.

I don't know why the story is not better known. Perhaps it is because its beneficiaries were the sons and daughters of some of the poorest and most neglected people on earth.

No further comment is needed from me on the extraordinary years of Jim Grant's leadership of UNICEF. But I would like to add a word to all those who have been involved with UNICEF over these years.

Jim Grant achieved what he did, as he said he would, by exerting leverage. And when the principles of leverage were first expounded 2,500 years ago, Archimedes summed it all up in one famous phrase: *'Give me a place to stand and I will move the world.'*

Jim's place to stand was UNICEF. He could not have done what he did standing in any other place. Not as an American politician, not as the head of a large non-governmental organization, not even as the head of any other UN agency. UNICEF is a household name in virtually every country of the world. It is a name that commands respect and affection everywhere. It is the name that opened the doors to Jim Grant. And it is the name that predisposed those inside those doors to listen.

The name of UNICEF, and all that it means, has been built up by a great many people – by those who work for UNICEF and by those who support it in almost every country of the world. All have been part of this story.

You built for Jim his place to stand. And he did move the world.

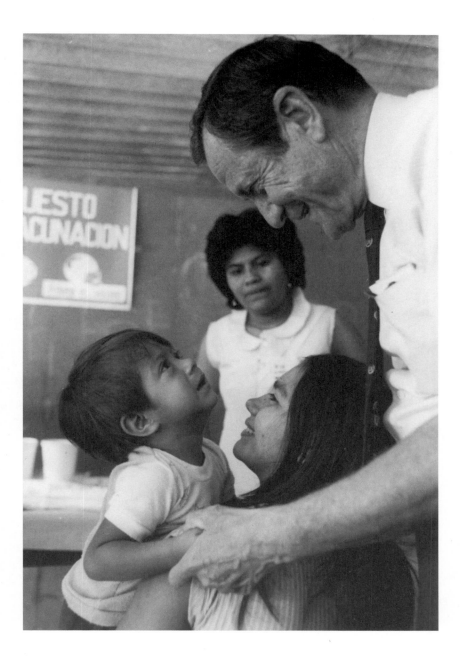

Jim Grant aged 6 with his Chinese nanny and his sister

Early influences in the life of James P. Grant

by Jon Rohde

'Ours is the first generation in history in which it is possible to think of bringing the benefits of civilization to all people.'
JAMES GRANT QUOTING ARNOLD TOYNBEE

James Pineo Grant was born in Peking (Beijing) in 1922, the grandson of a medical missionary and the son of John B. Grant, the Rockefeller Foundation's most noted public health specialist. His mother, devoted to family life, gave him his strong sense of optimism and self worth, instilling in him the belief that his engagement with social issues could indeed change the world. He grew up speaking fluent Mandarin, exploring the roads and alleys of the Chinese imperial capital with his friends, boys of better off Chinese families.

From an early age he accompanied his father on field trips to rural parts of China, especially to Ding Hsien. This rural county was where, with C. C. Chen, John B. Grant established the health care model for which he became known worldwide – the antecedent of the barefoot doctor movement which revolutionized primary health care some 35 years later.

Jim's father was committed to a system of health for all that would cost no more than one dollar per capita per year, the maximum that the peasants of that time could afford. Hence the emphasis was on health promotion, hygiene, home gardens for improved nutrition, and immunization. Health workers were recruited from the community in which they lived, the forerunners of Mao's barefoot doctors during the 1960s. Jim also recalled long train rides and endless conversations with Jimmy Yen, the champion of literacy for the masses, who saw reading as the means of liberating the poor from their feudal indenture to landholders. It was through such experiences that the young Jim Grant formed his view of development as a holistic process rooted in the right to land and the fruits of ones labour, and nurtured by knowledge and simple actions that liberate by freeing people from dependency and providing for their own health and well being.

Given his family history, one might have expected Jim to become a doctor. But he often recounted his grandfather's frustration in his small hospital in Ning Po where dealing with disease was like *'mopping up the floor under an overflowing sink without turning off the tap.'* And it was his own father who encouraged him to think about directing his efforts to helping turn off the tap of human suffering and stemming the constant flow of ill health. This was the concern that directed Jim's career towards public service and rural development, particularly land reform and public policies favouring employment.

Fluent in Chinese throughout his life, Jim was fondly remembered by many of those early friends who eventually came to lead the Chinese nation. I recall a very formal meeting in 1979 in the Great Hall of the People where Hua Huang, China's Foreign Minister, was lecturing the United States delegation on the evils of American imperialism and the virtues of Chinese Communist society. Jim was on the delegation, and pulled out a photograph of himself as a young American soldier holding the feet of a Chinese friend who was standing on his head – the young Hua Huang. The Foreign Minister laughed and the rest of the meeting became more of a true exchange. Jim brought people down to size, and had an easy way with everyone, be they peasants or heads of state.

But there were also tragic memories of his time in China. He recalled pedalling his bike to school in the cold Beijing winters when invariably a few had frozen to death sleeping along the sidewalks. And he used such examples to remind us that in the early part of this century suffering was widely accepted as the inevitable lot of the poor. Arriving in Calcutta in the spring of 1944, immediately after the great Bengal famine, he was appalled that the British government had done so little to relieve this massive tragedy even while the warehouses were full of grain. To be able to relieve suffering and not to do so was a grossly immoral act, he believed. Fifty years later the idea that morality must march with capacity was still one of his favourite themes.

Jim had a strong sense of history and referred to it often, for his life embraced some of the most important of events of the 20th century. As a young boy scout, he was camping at the Marco Polo Bridge when the Japanese invaded China; the thunder without rain turned out to be artillery fire, and at dawn his troop beat a quick retreat. In the Burma Theatre during World War II, his observation plane landed in a tree but he escaped his Japanese pursuers. He moved with Stillwell across the 'hump' becoming part of the US command in Chunking until the end of the war. Leaving the army, he was attached to George Marshall as work began on the Marshall plan for China's rehabilitation – a plan that was eventually scrapped and applied to Europe to great effect while China was mired in civil war.

Jim himself remained in China, working for the new United Nations Organization, and was joined there by his young wife, Ethel. At times they accompanied food and relief supplies to opposite sides of the nationalist-communist battle lines. As Chiang Kai Shek's forces fell, he dashed by chartered plane to Inner Mongolia to rescue Ethel, before fleeing to Taiwan along with the defeated nationalist government. There he became the Director of the Joint Commission on Rural Reconstruction, the major US-supported development agency that had been created with the aim of restructuring rural society mainly through giving land to peasants along with credit and training in new agricultural techniques. Over the years this strategy was applied across Taiwan to great effect, making the country in many ways a model of development through land reform, rural credit, education, and decentralized health services.

After the war, Jim attended Harvard Law School though he never intended to go into practice. He was convinced he needed to have his own safety net, for as a public sector employee he never wanted to be in a situation where he would have to compromise his own values. Public policy was his forte, and its application to the development of the poor his lifelong preoccupation. Law was his fall-back, a professional qualification that would enable him to stand up to bureaucracy and speak his mind even if it cost him his job. During law school summers he returned to China and to South East Asia in various capacities on behalf of the US Government. In 1950, as a representative of the National Student Association, he contacted such revolutionary leaders as Ho Chi Min, Sukarno, and scores of other less well know names who became friends for a lifetime. Jim was a networker.

In the 1960s Jim founded the Oversees Development Council, based in Washington D. C., as a 'think tank' to lobby and direct his own government in more appropriate and generous development activities. In the '60s and '70s, this independent NGO became a force that helped shape US policy towards the developing world. Among many innovations, he introduced new ways of measuring social progress – as opposed to purely economic development. Specifically, he promoted the Physical Quality of Life Index (PQLI) and the Disparity Reduction rate (DRR) as measures of social achievement – based on a combination of infant mortality, life expectancy, and literacy rates. At UNICEF, he continued to emphasize measurable human outcomes both in the statistical appendices to his annual report on the *State of the World's Children* and in the innovative league tables published in *The Progress of Nations*. *'If you can measure it,'* he often said, *'you have a better chance of holding people accountable.'*

As legal advisor in the US mission in Delhi in the early 1950s he helped broker a truce between India and Pakistan in Kashmir. The fact that this truce was short-lived was something that he regretted the rest of his life. Moving to become USAID Director in Sri Lanka, and later in Turkey, he nurtured the Green Revolution as a means of assuring self-reliance and empowering small farmers. He was always fascinated by the application of technology and its potential to change peoples lives, but realized that this potential depended not only on the technology itself but on social organization, communication, and well-supported dissemination – a challenge he took as his own.

All of this seemed in retrospect to be a preparation for the moment when, in 1979, he was appointed Executive Director of UNICEF.

Soon afterwards, we travelled together for several months in China and I convinced him of the 'doability' of a limited number of powerful, low-cost health technologies relating to the survival of children. Specifically these were: immunization, the use of oral rehydration against diarrhoea, and the underlying critical importance of good nutrition through breastfeeding and attention to growth of the young child. Clearly excited by the potential of these proven technologies (he named them GOBI for growth, oral rehydration, breastfeeding, and immunization), Jim immediately drew the analogy with the Green Revolution and formulated the idea of a Child Survival Revolution. The story of that revolution is told by many of his colleagues in the pages of this book.

I hope that this brief account of Jim Grant's early years will help to show the remarkable continuity of his vision and idealism. From his earliest recollections in the streets of Beijing to his last days as the head of UNICEF, Jim endeavoured to be an instrument that would help bring about Toynbee's vision. And to his last breath he remained true to the belief that his generation could be the first in history to bring the benefits of civilization to all of humankind.

The man behind the vision

by Richard Jolly

Jim Grant is today mostly remembered for his worldwide leadership for children. His 15 years as Executive Director of UNICEF was the crowning phase of his career, the period of challenge and fulfilment for which everything earlier in his life had been preparing him. This was his personal view which he sometimes mentioned to close friends. And certainly it was a view which many of us in UNICEF felt on many occasions, as Jim would present yet another challenge.

Jim was never satisfied, restless in exploring how to enlarge the world's vision for children, endlessly eager to work out one more doable solution to every problem which presented itself. I was speaking for many when at his memorial service I said that at least 25 million children were alive because of the worldwide actions which Jim Grant, through UNICEF and the United Nations, had set in motion.

Yet Jim Grant was much more than an advocate and global leader for children. He had a highly professional awareness of the broader issues of economic and social development on a global scale, a sophisticated grasp of the complex forces at work and, at the same time, a firm feel for the practical challenges of policy and strategy. He had founded and directed the Overseas Development Council in Washington, which from 1969 had led the way in the US and often worldwide in analysing problems of development from a policy perspective. Before this, Jim had held senior policy positions with USAID in Sri Lanka, Turkey, and Viet Nam as well as in Washington. He was never a dispassionate observer on the sidelines. From his youth in China, his college years in Berkeley organizing the 'Fair Bear' scheme to encourage students only to patronize shops which recognized minimum wage legislation, to his early defence of the communist regime in China and his skilful escape from questioning by McCarthy, Without being a radical, Jim was a freethinking committed supporter of the under-dog.

All this was often missed by those who only knew Jim as UNICEF's Executive Director. Many times I have heard people ask, *'Does Jim Grant really believe that third world exploitation can be ended with a few packets of oral rehydration salts?'* Jim Grant was miles in advance of such oversimplified beliefs. But Jim above all was a supreme tactician in getting things done, in making a difference, however unpromising the starting point. He concentrated his advocacy and mobilized UNICEF's actions for the doable agenda. At the same time, he never lost sight of the broader challenges. The oral rehydration packet, immunization, education for children, even the Child Survival and Development Revolution were early steps for jump-starting development, the pursuit of justice, equity and human progress on a global scale.

Jim always believed that the UN could and should be in the forefront of such a global movement.

Jim the development expert

My first clear memory of Jim as a development professional was in Algeria in 1976 at a presentation of a report to the club of Rome. The theme was 'Reshaping the International Order', a pre-occupation of the mid-1970s, in the aftermath of the oil crisis when the formation of OPEC – the Organisation of Petroleum Exporting Countries – had led to a 350 per cent increase in oil prices. Jim, with Mahbub ul Haq, had prepared a paper on 'Income Redistribution and the International Financing of Development'. Jim took the podium, one of a string of speakers exploring a crisis which had transferred two per cent of world income to the countries with oil but which in doing so had plunged the industrialized countries into recession and set back development in most of the NOPEC countries – those developing countries without oil.

Jim set out the broader view: longstanding injustice on a global scale, needing action, national and international. Global injustice had created the situation that OPEC was struggling to remedy. He argued his case using the analogy of South Africa, then under apartheid. In South Africa, the privileged whites formed about a fifth of South Africa's people, at that time about the same as the share of industrialized country population in total global population. The income of the whites in South Africa was about 80 per cent of South Africa's total national income – again about the same as the share of the industrialized countries in total world income. What should we learn from this, asked Jim?

In the case of South Africa, the causes of the inequalities were obvious. The structures of ownership and control which underlay apartheid – the police and army, the land, the mines and industry – were all dominated by the whites with the pass laws preventing free movement of blacks to the towns. Jim underlined the close parallels to the global economy – with the industrialized countries having an overwhelming dominance of armed force, of ownership of the means of global production, and with immigration laws to control the free movement of people. Jim drew his conclusion: we must look at the underlying structures maintaining global inequality and think strategically about how they can be changed.

It was a radical presentation, one of the most radical I ever heard from Jim. It showed his awareness of the roots of global inequality and his grasp of the deeper issues which in the long run must be tackled. Later in UNICEF, when I heard some outside critics asking whether Jim actually thought he could change the world with immunization and a few million ORT packets, I often thought back to Jim's speech in Algeria.

Three years later, in 1979, Jim was attending the UNICEF Executive Board in New York. I was also in New York, attending the UN Committee on Development Planning. Our task was to make suggestions for the goals and structure of the Third Development Decade, setting international priorities for the 1980s. This time I experienced a different Jim – the persistent advocate for global goals which would set the frame for a doable international agenda.

The time appeared ripe for exactly this sort of new initiative. Experience with the Second Development Decade in the 1970s suggested that the emphasis should shift from GNP goals for economic growth to more sectoral objectives. The eradication of smallpox, achieved in 1977, showed the potential of specific global targets. I was on the Committee charged with making specific proposals. And Jim was on the phone – each morning, before I left the hotel and each evening when I got back – asking what had been achieved. Although Jim had not yet been appointed Executive Director for UNICEF, he was actively seeking the post and obviously thinking ahead to the sort of goals he would find useful in UNICEF.

In the Committee of Development Planning, I was finding it very difficult to persuade my fellow committee members of the importance of having some specific goals and targets. The economists, the majority, wanted a focus on economic growth and what they saw as the big economic issues. Sectoral goals seemed less important. Most surprisingly, the WHO representative was dead against any further eradication goals. Smallpox, she argued, was unique. Nothing else was like it. This was before the eradication of polio or of guinea worm was on the agenda.

It was at that time that I learned what Jim meant by advocacy: specific proposals, marshalled in careful argument, an extraordinary attention to detail – and persistence. Not that I displayed much skill in the Committee – but Jim fed me the arguments, endlessly and specifically on the phone. It paid off. By the end of the meeting, the CDP Report recorded the need for the Third Development Decade strategy to include some long-run human goals related to life expectancy, infant mortality and possibly literacy and education. And Jim had laid some more of the foundations for his period as Executive Director of UNICEF. Only later would I realize what remarkable things could be achieved when Jim's vision and persistence were combined with the resources and organization of UNICEF.

A difficult honeymoon

Jim became Executive Director of UNICEF in January, 1980. His first two years were far from easy. With the success and the triumph of his later years, and the truly remarkable reputation UNICEF earned under his leadership, it was difficult to remember that there was ever a time when Jim had not been riding high. And during the memorial service in the Cathedral of St. John the Divine, when our hearts were heavy with his loss, it was not the occasion to recall the early difficulties.

But now probably is the moment, if only to emphasise the point that Jim's triumph did not come easily or without struggle and controversy. I saw this myself, three months before I joined UNICEF. Jim had invited me to the special meeting of the Executive Board being held in New York in October, 1981.

Jim had by then been Executive Director for one year and nine months. He had tried to take UNICEF by storm. He had called for new effort and new energy. *'We need to shift gears. We need to do more with less. We need to establish a think tank, to give UNICEF a brain.'* Staff morale had not been helped by a high level policy meeting Jim organized in Tarrytown and for which the main presentations had all been made by development experts from outside UNICEF. And to the Board, Jim proposed a new staff budget that seemed to call for 394 new posts (though many of these were in fact regularizing existing posts). The Board didn't like it – and many UNICEF staff, especially the old timers, felt that Jim was totally failing to appreciate UNICEF's already considerable reputation for practical action and cost effectiveness.

The special meeting of the Executive Board was called to discuss all this. Many Board Members were far from convinced and thought Jim was out of touch. By the end of the first day, there were even rumours in the corridors that Jim might have to resign.

With hindsight, this was the all time low. Jim showed that he could listen. He scaled down the budget. He showed more respect for UNICEF's strengths and past achievements. He planned future staff meetings, relying on UNICEF staff to give most of the inputs. But he never wavered in his determination to give the lead.

In retrospect, his effort to develop goals for children had been diverted in the first two years by several pre-occupations. One was the emergency in Kampuchea, for which UNICEF had taken on the lead agency role. This took an enormous amount of Jim's own time in mobilization, management and travel – at the cost of time and leadership for UNICEF's other programmes. Jim often said that such a lead agency role for UNICEF was one he was determined never to take on again though, in fact, he did in 1989 when specifically requested by the UN Secretary General to lead Operation Lifeline Sudan.

Another diversion came from the weak implementation of the Primary Health Care (PHC) programme agreed in Alma Ata. PHC had many virtues and was being jointly supported by WHO and UNICEF. Indeed, much of its approach and priorities had grown from UNICEF experience. But the casual and unfocused manner of follow up meant that business as usual rather than accelerated advance seemed likely. Jim was frustrated and sought more ambitious achievements.

In fact, initially, Jim thought that a major expansion of primary education should be UNICEF's priority for the 1980s. UNICEF would work in partnership with UNESCO to achieve a country by country programme of global expansion. In April 1982, Jim and several of us spent one full week in Paris, pressing the Director General of UNESCO to agree to such a programme. Jim hardly went outside UNESCO headquarters. But UNESCO totally lacked the vision and showed little response, being mainly interested in reaching an agreement that UNICEF would always turn to UNESCO whenever it needed consultants. So a global effort for educational expansion had to wait until 1990, when UNICEF and the World Bank, UNDP and UNESCO joined together in the Jomtien partnership for Education for All. Jim occasionally speculated how different the education record of the 1980s might have been had UNESCO responded positively in 1982.

The Child Survival and Development Revolution

This cleared the way for what became the Child Survival and Development Revolution. Already in 1981, Jim had started to emphasize, in speeches and in *The State of the World's Children Report*, the tragic and outrageous loss of life resulting from the very high child mortality rates. Jim spoke of the 40,000 children dying a day – and dramatized the figure by describing it as the equivalent of 120 Jumbo jets crashing each day, unimaginably horrifying but unnoticed.

In September, 1982, UNICEF organized a meeting of the North South Roundtable of the Society of International Development (SID), to explore what could be done. About thirty hand-picked participants were invited. In principle, the meeting focused on the problem of child malnutrition. But rapidly, it became clear that the causes of malnutrition and the causes of child mortality were closely aligned – and that there were low cost remedies, little used but readily available to tackle both problems. Jon Rohde made a gripping presentation, underlining the importance of immunization, holding up packets of Oral Rehydration Salts (ORS), explaining the importance of breastfeeding and waving a growth chart. Thus was born GOBI – the low cost, readily promoted four priorities: growth monitoring, oral rehydration, breast-feeding and immunization. If promoted worldwide, the four interventions could halve child mortality in a decade or two. Jim was convinced. Initially, this was presented as a programme for child survival – but soon it became the Child Survival and Development Revolution (CSDR), recognizing that survival and development went together.

Others in this volume have described the details of GOBI. How it became GOBI-FFF and accelerated child focused action in well over a hundred countries over the 1980s. My focus here is on Jim – how Jim elaborated the programme, directed it ever more closely to goals and set it within a broader frame of development action.

Several reinforcing actions took place in the mid-1980s. The first, in 1984, was to go to scale. This was already the challenge within each country. How UNICEF could support GOBI not only as a set of activities but as a programme designed to reach every child in the country. Colombia showed the way. In 1984, with the enthusiastic support of President Betancur, himself a surviving child of a large family in which most of his brothers and sisters had died early. A campaign for mass immunization was launched, with support from the Catholic Church, the Red Cross, the police, the labour unions, the Boy Scouts and the entire school network. The crusade reached some 800,000 children, immunizing them on three separate days, each one month apart. The effort raised immunization coverage to about 75 per cent at a time when coverage in developing countries averaged 20 per cent or less. Several elements were developed to ensure sustainability. Learning about GOBI was made a part of the secondary school curriculum, with local service to promote GOBI actions being made a practical component. The Catholic Church linked GOBI to the catechism, to make learning about child health part of the preparations for bringing up a child in the ways of God.

The expansion of immunization was underway – and efforts in Burkina Faso, Senegal and districts of India and Nigeria soon were added. Turkey then became the big demonstration that nationwide coverage was possible. The Prime Minister, Turgut Ozal, was already a good friend of Jim from their days together when Jim was the USAID Representative for Turkey in the mid 1960s. So in mid-1985, school teachers were asked to end their vacations three weeks early in order to come back to their villages and act as the mobilizers and activist leaders for a nationwide immunization campaign. The success was remarkable. Immunization levels soared from under 20 to 84 per cent. The campaign had also promoted the use of ORT. The revolutionary potential of social mobilization in support of the CSDR had been demonstrated.

With these experiences in hand, Jim was ready to put the major challenge. Could UNICEF take on global leadership to achieve worldwide the goal of 80 per cent coverage of immunization? *'Should we take this on?'* asked Jim to a specially convened senior leadership meeting. Jim knew what answer he expected – as did everyone in the room. Still, I thought someone should raise the unspoken thought, so I asked, *'And what will we do to UNICEF's reputation if we fail?'* Someone accused me of sabotage, even suggesting I should be shot! Jim got his assent. The WHO-UNICEF goal of universal immunization was now accepted as a serious priority for UNICEF and WHO to support and to do all possible to achieve.

Mobilizing for goals – and for their achievement

The importance of repeating this oft told story about GOBI, immunization and ORT is to make clear the difference between a UN agency supporting another good goal in principle – and seriously mobilizing to achieve it. Many an agency declares general support for great goals adopted by the international community, occasionally even fervent support. Jim Grant showed how to achieve them.

Support which led to achievement required the adoption of the goals as a specific and major institutional priority to be taken seriously in every UNICEF country office – backed up with encouragement, technical support, resources and monitoring. Building UNICEF-wide commitment to the GOBI goals and the immunization target took time and persuasion. It took much more than simply sending a clear instruction from headquarters and from the regional offices, though this was done. UNICEF had a long tradition of 'the country programme approach', developing a five year country programme with priorities defined by the country in relation to children's needs and priorities in the local situation. Many field staff at first felt the country programme approach was totally inconsistent with formulating any global or institution-wide priority, another battle Jim had to fight.

Technical support meant the organization of a series of regional meetings, to go over the issues, to study and learn from success and failure and to build understanding and commitment.

Then came resources. The priorities for GOBI and the CSDR did not mean the abandonment of all other concerns for children, or of the country programme approach. But broad guidelines had to be formulated. It was decided that UNICEF offices should spend 80 per cent of their country programme resources in the priority areas of CSDR, supporting catalytic national actions to reduce child mortality, applied to whichever areas of action seemed most necessary and effective in the country concerned.

Even with this priority, many UNICEF offices would find themselves with insufficient programme resources. Some additional 'global resources' were therefore made available from central funds. Although never more than 5 per cent of total UNICEF programme expenditure, global funds always remained a flashpoint of controversy with the field. Although Jim left it to his staff largely to devise and carry out the elements of this country support, he never wavered in his strategic support for these mechanisms of support and of the decisions of his staff in carrying them out.

Adjustment with a human face

It is easy to forget the most difficult economic context in which all this took place. The 1980s began with world recession, followed by the debt crisis in Mexico, with serious repercussions in most parts of the developing world, but especially in Latin America and sub-Saharan Africa. Education and health budgets were being slashed as a consequence of the economic difficulties, reinforced by the harsh nature of the structural adjustment programmes that the World Bank and the IMF were pressing on countries.

All this was reported on and debated in the UN's Administrative Coordinating Committee (ACC) which met every four months or so and which brought together the heads of all the UN agencies and a few other senior UN staff. The ACC was one of the few occasions when the heads of the World Bank and the IMF would meet with their senior UN colleagues. Usually, the Bank and the IMF presented their view of the global economic situation, after which they would leave, perhaps first listening politely to a few of the comments offered by some of the more senior UN leaders.

This is when Jim started emphasizing the human consequences of adjustment, especially for children. Unlike others in the ACC, Jim rarely had a written statement prepared in advance. He relied on one or two of us in support to suggest speaking points in response to the flow of debate. Jim then drew on his own sophisticated knowledge of development to construct a powerful and relevant reply. Thus was born the call for an alternative to orthodox adjustment.

It was initially M. Delarosiere, Managing Director of the IMF, who responded. He invited Jim down to Washington for a full morning of discussion with him as well as his deputy and a young note-taker. Three of us went with Jim, armed only with an outline for an alternative approach. This ten page paper had been written over two days in the previous week. We joked as we walked to the marble palace which forms the IMF that we felt like David marching to battle with Goliath, armed with nothing but a sling and a small stone of conscience and concern for children.

After pleasantries, Jim opened. Even here, he could not miss his chance to make a sales pitch for ORT. He summarized the 4 million deaths a year from diarrhoea, explained how an ORS packet could deal with two thirds of the problem – and rammed home the point with a triumphant – *'and all in a ten cent packet.'* Delarosiere was duly impressed, especially by the enormity of the contrast between the deaths which could be avoided and the cost which was so small as to be invisible to all but the cleaning staff of the IMF.

At this point, Jim handed over to me. I explained the logic of adjustment with a human face: ensure that children and child nutrition were protected during structural adjustment. Could one really claim to be restoring a country's economy if at the end of adjustment, malnutrition had risen and school enrolments had fallen? One needs adjustment which helps people, not harms them. *'Give me an example of a country which has done this,'* Delarosiere asked. I replied, almost without thinking, *'Great Britain during the second world war.'* It was a good example, since it was one which someone from an industrialized country could readily relate to. During the second world war, Britain had to halve its imports even while restructuring industry to expand military production. Yet even while doing this as a matter of the most urgent war-time priority, in a war originally expected to last months rather than years, Britain under Churchill protected the health and nutrition and education of its whole population so well that at the end of the war the nutritional status of the British population was higher than ever before.

This was Adjustment with a Human Face. Jim was totally at home with the argument, using the ORS packet and other low cost aspects of GOBI to show that UNICEF had operational specifics ready for implementation – but always ready to the elaborate the economic argument in conceptual terms. A year later in 1985, Jim helped promote Adjustment with a Human Face to a wider audience. I gave the Barbara Ward Memorial Lecture at the SID global conference in Rome and Jim introduced me. From that moment, Adjustment with a Human Face took off. UNICEF issued the lecture as a booklet and two years later published a substantial book on the theme, in which the basic arguments were developed and elaborated by economists Andrea Cornia and Frances Stewart.

This is a piece about Jim and UNICEF, not about Adjustment with a Human Face. But the two were linked and it may be useful to suggest why. One of the reasons why Adjustment with a Human Face was so readily accepted, even in time, by the Bank and the IMF, was, in my view, that it was backed by Jim and UNICEF. Jim was the passionate advocate, utterly convincing in his commitment to get things done. Adjustment with a Human Face complemented the practical specifics of ORT, immunization and the rest of GOBI. It showed Jim and UNICEF master of a full development agenda, from the specifics of saving a child's life to the strategic economics for building a better future for children and their families over the longer term.

Jim was aware of the exceptional difficulties facing most countries of sub-Saharan Africa throughout the 1980s: debt, drought, destabilization and the unrelenting pressures to adopt policies of austerity and adjustment. This led Jim to ensure that UNICEF gave special priority to sub-Saharan Africa in the use of its own resources and in its global advocacy. Jim never wavered in his belief that, in spite of all, the situation of children could be improved in these desperately poor countries. Events proved him right. In spite of declines by one tenth in per capita incomes and many other setbacks, child mortality was clearly reduced over the 1980s. Not as fast as in other regions, but by a clear margin.

The World Summit for Children

By 1989, the Child Survival and Development Revolution was well under way. Immunization coverage had soared in more than a hundred countries. Over 60 of them were on track to achieve 80 per cent coverage in each of the six antigens, which had been defined as the effective measure of universal coverage. The battle was not, of course, won. There were still doubts and uncertainties. But one could imagine that victory would be achieved. Jim of course was already asking 'what next?'

In 1988, Jim used The State of the World's Children Report to float an idea. What about a World Summit for Children? For all his bold leadership and willingness to take risks, Jim ensured the tentative proposal was worded with great care.

'The time may therefore be ripe to consider a meeting of heads of state – or perhaps a Special Session of the United Nations General Assembly – in order to discuss and prepare for action on the great opportunities for protecting today's children – and tomorrow's world.'

Now, with seven summit meetings held in the decade since the World Summit for Children of 1990, it may be difficult to imagine any reason why Jim, the supreme risk-taker, would hesitate. But no world summit of any size had ever been held until that time. We would joke that the last one had been the Congress of Vienna marking the end of the Napoleonic War in 1815. It was not clear that the idea of a summit would be taken seriously or that more than a handful of heads of state would come. And there were difficulties and sensitivities within the UN. Several times we were advised by UN officials that no UN meeting could be held to which only heads of state would be invited. Governments alone could decide the level at which they chose to be represented.

Until only a few weeks before the summit was about to begin, it was also argued that there was no way in which seating in the ECOSOC chamber could be changed to accommodate heads of state around a single large square table. This raised again the question as to how many would come. Finally agreement was reached on having a large square table but the number of heads of state likely to come remained a matter of real dispute. To relieve the tensions being created, Jim launched a bet. Who could guess closest the number of heads of state who would actually turn up? I was in charge of the kitty – and the one dollar bets were held in strict confidence. But now I can reveal them. Of the 35 persons or so who put down their dollar, Jim's own estimate was highest at 53. Even this was 18 below the number of heads of state who actually arrived: 71.

The real part of the preparation was of course the Declaration and Plan of Action. For Jim this was the purpose of the Summit. To get commitments to goals and a plan of action that would extend the success of immunization and the Child Survival and Development Revolution into a wider range of actions and activities, directed to the core of children's and women's needs throughout the world. There was also the Convention on the Rights of the Child to build on. After eight years of prolonged negotiation, the text had finally been agreed in 1989. It needed ratification by 20 individual countries to become internationally recognized. And to become effective at national level, countries needed to ratify it individually. The Summit Declaration called for each country to take such action.

The Summit took place in the UN on the last day of September 1990, attended by 71 heads of state or government and representatives of nearly 100 other countries. It ran like clockwork. In fact it ran slightly ahead of time for most of the day, since the photograph of the heads of state was so skilfully organized that the whole photo session was completed in eight minutes. Each head of state was then guided into the General Assembly by a child from his or her country, with the child holding a flag of the country to ensure rapid identification. At the end of the day, eight children read out the Declaration and afterwards children carried the signature books from each head of state to the front.

Such was the ritual. The excitement and sense of occasion was truly impressive. But Jim was looking far beyond. Now he had both goals for the 1990s and commitments at the highest level of government. He also had the success of immunization and what it showed about the possibilities of making further rapid advances for children, even given economic constraints and the setbacks of debt and structural adjustment. Child mortality rates had fallen in all regions of the world over the 1980s and in virtually every country. Over a period when income per capita had been stagnant in Latin America and had declined by more a tenth in sub-Saharan Africa, the reductions in child mortality were unprecedented. Jim called them a minor miracle.

The 1990s were the years for mobilizing behind the new commitments. Every UNICEF office encouraged the government in its country to prepare, on its own or with NGOs and others, a National Plan of Action (NPA), explaining how the summit goals would be implemented in their country. Some 150 countries prepared such NPAs, including a number of industrialized countries. Again this was an unprecedented response in the UN where most development declarations are thought in fact to refer only to developing countries.

Jim then mobilized himself. Armed with a colour-coded chart for each country, he toured the world, visiting as many heads of state as he could see, to argue the case for accelerated action. The charts showed the situation for each goal for each country, with regional comparisons. Green indicated that for that particular goal, in that particular country progress was on track for success. Yellow, that extra effort was required. Red meant danger – that the goal was very unlikely to be achieved without extra special action. Jim would illustrate his point with an 'oomph', looking up at the head of state and indicating with a smile and body language that the goal was still achievable but only with the personal commitment and effort of the highest level of national leadership.

On such occasions, Jim's charm and persuasive powers were extraordinary. No one, not even the most cynical or hard bitten politician could doubt Jim's sincerity or question his appeal to their better nature and to their self interest as political leaders. They realized that what was publicly good for their nation's children was good for their own reputations.

But even with these powerful personal contacts, Jim left nothing to chance. Before leaving the country concerned, no matter how short or long the visit, Jim made sure that draft letters were prepared to the head of state and each of the ministers he had seen. These letters were no short 'thank you' notes. Rather they were a point by point summary of all the specific requests Jim had made, with summaries of the promises made and how important they would be for their positive impact on the nation's children. These letters would of course be prepared by the UNICEF office. But Jim would work over each and every one, ensuring that they rose to the specifics of the occasion. They would be signed before Jim departed, often when Jim was climbing aboard the plane!

Many times in the UN I have heard people admiringly talk of Jim Grant's persuasive powers but then add, as if in explanation, that Jim had the easy mandate. *'Who could be against children?'* it was often said. Or, *'Jim was pushing at an open door.'* This is not my impression or that of others who worked closely with him. And to say this is to miss the real lessons of Jim's commitment, advocacy and organization. Jim mobilized for children, but with concentrated attention to generating support for specific doable goals – reducing deaths from diarrhoea, eradicating polio by immunization, cutting deaths from measles, getting all girls and boys in school, encouraging all countries to ratify the Convention on the Rights of the Child.

Jim was a master of motivation and incentive. Before he arrived in any country, he had written in his pocket notebook the actual number of child deaths that year in that country, with an estimate of how many had died from each cause. He talked in terms of child deaths, not mortality rates, since the first was human and immediate, the latter technical and remote. He would use child mortality rates when he wanted to make comparisons with other countries – often to show how another country was doing better, even with less resources. Such comparisons were made to motivate, not to humiliate. So though Jim might point to the tragedy of high numbers of child deaths, he would use the example of a better nearby country to demonstrate that rapid progress was possible – to explain how it could be achieved.

Jim – leader and manager

Jim is not usually thought of as a manager, at least not a good one. Indeed, Jim was sometimes criticised precisely for his failures in management. I think his record deserves another look, from a management point of view.

The 1990 achievement of universal immunization in the developing world was an unprecedented feat. It was achieved only by an extraordinary effort of global planning and decentralized mobilization involving heads of state, ministries of health, churches, Rotarians and other NGOs, supported by UNICEF offices, WHO, aid donors and other parts of the UN and international community. Over the twelve months of 1990, a hundred million children were brought six or more times to clinics or immunizing stations in some 150 countries, with public announcements made, vaccines delivered, immunizing services made ready, records kept. Jim referred to this as the largest effort of peacetime mobilization ever achieved. Is this an example of poor management?

Over Jim's fifteen years at the helm of UNICEF goal oriented programming was developed and revenue and expenditure rose fourfold, from some $250 million to over $1,000 million. UNICEF's reputation rose to unprecedented heights, higher than any other part of the UN. In Europe, one survey showed that UNICEF achieved over 90 per cent name recognition, all but 5 per cent positive. Are these signs of poor management?

Jim died on 28 January,1995, about two weeks after he had resigned from UNICEF. There was an outpouring of sympathy from heads of state and senior figures in most countries of the world. Two and a half thousand persons crowded into the Cathedral of St John the Divine in New York for a memorial meeting. It was estimated that because of the Child Survival Revolution mobilized by UNICEF under Jim Grant, some 25 million children were alive who would otherwise be dead. Is this a sign of poor management?

Jim was sometimes said to be a poor manager because he listened too little and talked too much. There was some truth in this – though less than many who did not know him well often thought. Jim was an advocate and promoter supreme. He had honed these skills over many years, indeed from college days when he had paid his way through university at Berkeley by operating the Coca Cola franchise. But Jim could and did listen, especially in the presence of those with first hand experience or clear research findings that he felt would be valuable for the cause of children. Then Jim would listen intensely, pressing for ever more detail until he was sure he had fully understood.

But Jim was not good at small talk, at least during the final two decades of his life. He was focused on action – and he was not prepared to waste time listening if he spotted an opportunity to mobilize for action.

Jim could also be infuriating in not getting to the point, especially when it was someone else's point and Jim wanted to stick to some different topic. In this sense his single minded focus and management focus was often bought at a high price, perhaps an unnecessarily high price, to others.

And Jim could be infuriating for his ability to repeat the message, over and over and over and over again. It is true he repeated himself with skill and subtlety, almost always with new twists and minor variations. But those of us in his core management team often suffered. Yet Jim Grant knew that in a bureaucracy like the UN, to get the message across requires repetition. I myself have seen many heads of UN agencies who state a message once and think that they have got their point across. Once mentioned, they are ready to turn to a new topic. Jim knew better. Only by strategic repetition could he get his messages across. High rates of child mortality are unnecessary and totally unacceptable in the world today. Many low cost approaches are readily available. But to get them applied requires goals, focused action and widespread mobilization. This requires many repetitions of the message.

Choosing his leaders

Jim's approach to management relied heavily on selecting leaders who shared a deep commitment to his vision and goals. He needed people who had demonstrated the capacity to get things done. Thus, he always insisted on his own close personal involvement in the selection of his country representatives or any others of his senior staff. These selections were formally made by the senior staff review committee, which he chaired. For appointments, the critical test for Jim was the ability to deliver.

Related to this pre-occupation with leadership, was Jim's skilful resistance to pressures from UN member governments to take aboard one of their own nationals, often into senior staff positions. Such pressures are only too common in the United Nations and they are often identified as a major cause of UN inefficiency and poor performance. Before I joined the UN and had first hand experience of these pressures, I had imagined they mostly came from developing countries. My experience in UNICEF showed exactly the opposite. In four cases out of five or even more, the pressures on appointments came from donor countries, who somehow felt that since they were financing a disproportionate share of the UN they had a right to nominate their nationals.

Jim was very skilful in dealing with these pressures, rarely in my experience giving in to them. Given the UN's financial dependence on the richer countries, and, in the case of the funding agencies like UNICEF, their high dependence on a core of key donors, saying no required skill and explanation.

But Jim did accept that the donors who made the larger contributions to its total budget deserved some larger share of their nationals in UNICEF's total staffing. After one or two mistakes, this was allowed for by moving to a transparent system, under which a donor could expect a share in UNICEF's staffing equal to about half of its share in UNICEF's revenue. (The other half provided for staffing from developing countries, who could not be expected to contribute in a major way to UNICEF's budget.) But recognizing the case for a country to have a higher share of staff carried no rights to nominate particular nationals to UNICEF. Rather, it carried an obligation on UNICEF to ensure that following its normal staff procedures, and without lowering its recruiting standards in any way, the proportion of staff from under represented nations would gradually be increased.

A similar procedure was followed with respect to improving the gender balance in UNICEF's staffing. A review of the male-female balance in the mid-1980s showed that women formed only about a quarter of UNICEF's professional staff, both because initial recruitment was biased and, even worse, because promotion rates had long favoured men, even when women were more qualified, more experienced and spoke more languages. Jim rapidly agreed to the setting of targets – the key goal being that by 1990, 33 per cent of international professionals should be women. When this goal was achieved, a new target was set. That by 1995, 40 per cent of international professional posts should be held by women. This target was also achieved, without any compromise of standards in appointment or promotions. For many of us, it was another example of the importance of setting goals and the ability of an institution to achieve them, providing leadership gives steady attention to them.

An opposite but revealing characteristic was Jim's attitude to staff who were not performing adequately. This was not a frequent occurrence but when it arose, Jim always reacted in the same way. What has been done, he would ask, to guide or support the person in question? And even about persons who seemed to be in a post beyond their capacity to deliver, Jim would ask, what is being done to build the person's strengths and capacities, to help the person to grow? Such reactions were an amalgam of many elements: loyalty and commitment to his senior staff, a reluctance to admit an earlier wrong choice – but above all a deep and almost endless faith in people and belief in their capacity to change. Of course, some called this soft management. Others of us called it human and humane.

Mobilizing and sharing resources

Jim's belief in these human qualities underlay his approach to mobilization for children. This was also a critical component of his management style. There was no way UNICEF could directly implement any of the goals for children or even its global programmes. UNICEF, as Jim would often say, was a handful of people with a bagful of pennies. The challenge was to use these scarce resources to mobilize a worldwide movement for children, to go to scale in ways that would achieve a global impact. The achievement of 80 per cent coverage of immunization was only one of a number of goals – but it provides a perfect illustration. UNICEF could not and did not directly undertake any of the actual immunizations, let alone undertake or support most of the other actions needed to build up the interest, the knowledge and the participation of all the many millions of people involved. But it happened by a conscious process of mobilization – with UNICEF's handful of people and its bagful of money being used catalytically.

Jim also used his personal charisma and commitment, with that of his senior colleagues, to show the way and mobilize further interest. As with Jim's management of UNICEF's own staff, Jim assumed the best of those he was trying to persuade to join the bandwagon or to give their own leadership. He believed, that innate to all people was a sympathy and potential caring for children. Jim's challenge was to show doable ways in which this potential could be released and brought into play, at sufficiently low cost as to survive other competing pressures.

Following this principle, Jim persuaded many heads of state to get personally involved in their national programmes for children, for example in their immunization by being photographed giving polio drops to a baby. He mobilized the drivers of UNICEF vehicles by ensuring they had the training to be good and informed advocates for child nutrition. He expanded the UNICEF goodwill ambassador programme, appealing to the volunteer spirit and human commitments of Audrey Hepburn, Liv Ullman, Peter Ustinov and other figures from the film and sporting world. And Jim seized on the bright-eyed idealism of millions of children themselves to appeal to their willingness to be young advocates for children and undertake actions which would save lives and give children a better future.

Collaboration with other parts of the UN

Many thought that Jim was so committed to UNICEF and children that he had little time for the rest of the UN. This was almost the opposite of the truth. In the ACC, Jim consistently displayed a vision for the whole UN and argued passionately for UN-wide actions for poverty reduction, basic human needs and for UN leadership to respond better to adjustment and debt reduction. The needs of sub-Saharan Africa and of the least developed countries elsewhere were a priority he often underlined, always with a note of hope and an emphasis on doability.

In areas more directly related to health and children, Jim forged very close links with WHO. When the Italians offered UNICEF $100 million for nutrition, Jim argued that this should be made a joint programme with WHO, with some sharing of resources. On several occasions when Congress was about to offer UNICEF an increase in funding, Jim argued that part of the proposed increase should be given to UNDP. I was present in the mid-1980s, when Jim had a meeting with Jean Ripert, then UN Director General for Development and apart from the Secretary General, the highest-ranking civil servant of the UN. Jean Ripert said that he had heard UNICEF described as the least collaborative of the UN agencies. Far from being defensive, Jim said he took such criticism extremely seriously. He said that when President Carter had nominated him for the post of Executive Director of UNICEF, the President had said that if at the end of his time in UNICEF, the UN as a whole was not stronger, Jim should consider himself to have failed.

Jim never wavered in this commitment to collaboration. During 1980-95, UNICEF took the lead in many initiatives of collaboration – strengthening collaboration with WHO, actively supporting and expanding coordinating groups among the funding agencies, for nutrition, education, water and sanitation and UN programmes in general and encouraging the creation of a humanitarian and emergency coordinating group. But coordination, like beauty, is in the eye of the beholder and notwithstanding these initiatives and actions, UNICEF was and still is often seen as the agency less willing to coordinate its activities with others. Why?

For Jim, and for UNICEF, coordination was for a purpose, especially towards goals. Co-ordination was valued if it enhanced and speeded up action, but not if it slowed things down.

The ability to act quickly using its own resources did not always endear UNICEF to other agencies, whose own budgets and procedures often did not allow for speedy action. Sometimes, UNICEF was even accused of going fast simply to show up the others. And UNICEF's good public image was often held against it. Many times, I heard Jim tell his staff: *'Give others the credit,'* or even *'Leave UNICEF's name out of it.'* One of his favourite morals was, *'Never under-estimate the amount of good a person can do if they do not mind who gets the credit.'* Sometimes, on hearing that another UN agency was supporting a key action for children, Jim would instruct that UNICEF should issue a press release in support but make no mention of UNICEF's actions in the same area, lest we appear to be stealing the other agency's thunder.

Jim's final words

Jim's final statement to UNICEF's Executive Board was a memorable occasion. Of course, he had a written statement prepared before the meeting by his own staff. But moved by some of the comments and statements in the last session, Jim started drafting feverishly, as others spoke. I have a copy of his handwritten four pages. They read as follows.

'With the possibility that this may be my last meeting with the Executive Board, let me take this opportunity to express my appreciation for the privilege of serving as Executive Director over the past 15 years.

As I have said before, over my lifetime I have been guided by certain principles which I believe are very much those that have been underlying UNICEF's work. Foremost among these has been the principle so aptly captured by Arnold Toynbee: 'Our age is the first since the dawn of history in which mankind dared to believe it practical to make the benefits of civilization available to the whole of the human race.'

That is what UNICEF has been doing since its new incarnation in 1950. And our year 2000 goals, if we achieve them, will really represent having crossed the watershed toward meeting the most essential needs of the great majority of the world's children and giving all children a far more equal start in life.

Second, that there is an urgency to our work. Morality does march with changing capacity. As Primo Levi has said: 'If we can relieve torment and do not, we become the tormentors.'

Since 1950, we have seen global per capita GNP more than double, the invention of such low cost interventions as the vaccines for polio and measles and oral rehydration therapy for the dehydration of children, a vast increase in the world's social mobilization and informational capacity – radio, TV, literacy and schools...UNICEF has represented a major force for bringing this change in capacity to relieve torment to the attention of the world.

It was Bernard Shaw who said 'You see things; and you say why? But I dream things that never were; and I say why not?'

It has been my privilege to be Executive Director of UNICEF during an era when it has dreamed and asked 'why not' a child survival revolution? And 5 million fewer children die annually as a result.

UNICEF dreamed of the world's first truly global summit to be convened for children and asked why not? The result has been an unprecedented summit and a World Summit for Children Declaration and Plan of Action for the decade of the 1990s.

UNICEF dreamed of a Convention on the Rights of the Child which would be the most comprehensive and complex of any human rights convention in history, and asked why not – and later dreamed of it being the first ever universally ratified convention, and asked why not? The result: the most ratified human rights convention ever – ratified by 166 countries – and a 1995 target for universal ratification.

We have had the satisfaction of seeing the Cairo International Conference for Population and Development declare a new holistic approach to population which largely embraces goals framed by the World Summit for Children for achievement by the year 2000.

We have the satisfaction of looking forward to the World Social Summit which should give additional impetus to our work for children.

Distinguished delegates, the world has never before set a framework of detailed goals to be achieved in a decade. To date, the progress has been satisfying – a majority of countries will achieve a majority of the 13 goals set for mid-decade. The real test of course, will be the year 2000.

Madame President, there are only 324 weeks until the end of December 2000. I can think of no better way of marking the new millennium than to be meeting the most essential needs of all our children.'

Building foundations
for the castles in the air

by Nyi Nyi

If you have built castles in the air, your work need not be lost;
that is where they should be.
Now put the foundations under them.

HENRY DAVID THOREAU, *WALDEN*

Jim Grant's 15 year tenure as Executive Director marked the rise of UNICEF to an unprecedented level of achievement and global recognition. Under his leadership, the organization became known as the dynamic agency of the United Nations system dedicated exclusively to children and development. Mr. Grant became known both in developing and industrialized countries as the untiring advocate and ambassador for children and social development. He was admired for his uncommon mix of idealism, vision, practical commitment and effective leadership. UNICEF earned a reputation as a caring and effective 'doer' organization which delivered through its dedicated staff, located mostly in developing countries. Its support broadened and the revenue jumped from about $250 million to over $1 billion during his tenure.

Within UNICEF, James P. Grant became known as 'JPG' — a term used by junior and senior colleagues alike. He was also called affectionately the 'Fearless Leader' by many of his colleagues.

JPG was greatly influenced by his father, John B. Grant, MD, a revolutionary medical and social thinker. Dr. Grant was the founder of the first schools of public health in Beijing and Calcutta where he emphasized the equal importance of education and health in public health activities. Dr. Grant also instilled in his son the importance of integrating biological and medical sciences with social organization in programme delivery. He knew that medical advances do not reach the poor by any automatic process of diffusion, but must be made available by a conscious and sustained effort to bridge the gap between what science knows and what people need.

Having lived and also worked for most of his life for the developing world, JPG understood the resource limitations, as well as the dynamics of developing societies, especially their cultural and political sensitivities and nuances. He had a fine sense of persuasion, which usually got positive results without offending people's sensitivities. Based on his experience in China and Sri Lanka, he developed the concept of positive deviance. His involvement in the Green Revolution in Turkey in the 1960s provided him with the experience of 'going to scale'. He was also conscious of the potential of the evolving communications revolution of the '80s and early '90s and the ability of new media to reach people in all strata of society.

When JPG took over the leadership of UNICEF in 1980 he felt that, to be more effective, UNICEF had to accelerate and move beyond the confines of projects covering a few limited areas with a limited number of activities. These would not provide enough traction to really change national policies and practices. There was also the problem that such projects were not likely to be sustained once the project was terminated. Because of the limitation of resources compared to needs, he also felt the need to leverage the power of ideas. His hope was to create a 'think tank' to define and promote a children's agenda in the market place of ideas. He also argued that a children's agenda could be a Trojan horse leading to broader social and human development – a sine qua non for development. However, UNICEF's governing body, the Executive Board did not approve the idea of creating a think tank. It was too radical a departure from the established culture of UNICEF, which is essentially one of programme delivery.

The Child Survival and Development Revolution

In September 1982, the deliberations in a seminar focussed on nutrition broadened to explore the challenges for children and for UNICEF. The emphasis shifted to what was doable and could achieve traction to accelerate the agenda for children, especially in the current difficult times. The discussions led to the development of a strategy later to become known as the 'Child Survival Revolution' – where the primary objective was to halve the 40,000 daily deaths of children under five years of age and improve their nutritional status. It included four simple, low cost and doable elements – growth monitoring, oral rehydration therapy (ORT), breastfeeding and immunization. This was commonly known as GOBI, an acronym given by a participant of the seminar, John Evans, the then Director of Population, Health and Nutrition of the World Bank. Two elements (food supplementation and family or birth spacing) were added the following year. Female education was added still later and the acronym became GOBI-FFF and thestrategy was later renamed 'Child Survival and Development Revolution' (CSDR) to incorporate broader developmental aspects of the child.

The elements of CSDR were not new to UNICEF. The early work on growth monitoring in Nigeria, pioneered by David Morley of the London Institute of Child Health, was successfully used as an indicator of the health of a child. UNICEF has always taken a strong interest in breastfeeding and, in 1979, was the co-sponsor, with the World Health Organization, of the Conference on Infant and Young Child Feeding. This led to the adoption of the International Code on Marketing of Breastmilk Substitutes by the World Health Assembly in 1981.

The two principal elements of CSDR aimed at achieving the original goal of halving infant and child deaths soon became oral rehydration therapy and immunization. These, together with acute respiratory infections, were the three principal killers of children under five. At the time, diarrhoea was the principal child killer, accounting for over 4 million deaths per year out of the annual total of 15 million deaths under five. Sadly, 70 per cent of these deaths could have been prevented by oral rehydration therapy. It was estimated that the other element – immunization – could easily prevent 3.4 million vaccine preventable deaths. These two interventions became areas of focal attention, leading to Peter McPherson, Administrator of the US Agency for International Development naming them 'twin engines' of child survival. Control of acute respiratory infections was not included at the time because it involved the administration of antibiotics whose use was not allowed to non-medical practitioners in many developing countries.

Immunization later became the principal thrust of CSDR and achieving the goal of universal child immunization (UCI) by 1990 soon became the primary focus of child survival. Various hypotheses were advanced about the priority given to accelerating immunization over other interventions. The general consensus was that there was a human urge to take quantitative targets as a challenge since progress on measurable targets is more visible and stimulating. In fact, JPG lost a bet to Robert McNamara who was of the opinion that immunization would be the fastest mover, while JPG felt ORT would be the front runner.

The Expanded Programme on Immunization (EPI) was established in 1974 as a sequel to the conquest of small pox, although the last case of small pox was not reported until October 1977 from Somalia.

In May 1977, the World Health Assembly set a global goal for universal child immunization of six basic antigens for under-ones by the year 1990. This resolution was reaffirmed in 1986.

Although the goal was set initially in 1977, progress was slow and the general feeling was that unless the programme was accelerated, the goal was unlikely to be achieved. In 1974, the coverage for any of the vaccines was estimated by WHO to be less than five per cent. By 1983, some progress was made showing the coverage for a third dose of DPT vaccine among infants in the developing world in the order of 30 per cent, falling to 24 per cent for a third dose of polio and to 14 per cent for measles immunization. However, the situation changed once child survival was incorporated by UNICEF as a principal thrust under the leadership of JPG. His untiring efforts to mobilize the world for UCI completely altered priorities, prospects and expectations.

By 1984-85, immunization rates had doubled or even trebled in several countries. The worldwide demand for vaccines in 1985 was three times higher than that of 1983 resulting in a corresponding reduction of child deaths from vaccine-preventable diseases. JPG had the idea of mobilizing on an even greater scale. So in June 1985, at his urging, the United Nations Secretary General, Javier Perez de Cuellar, wrote to the presidents and prime ministers of 159 member states of the United Nations calling their attention to this important drive. A resolution in support of UCI was also passed at the 1985 UN General Assembly, joined by 74 governments and over 400 volunteer organizations.

The UCI was now in full swing and JPG was the master strategist, providing effective leadership which would put him and UNICEF on the map and on the road to a string of successes.

Strategic elements

Having now found a wedge to pierce the armour of 'business as usual', JPG adopted a twin strategic approach of CSDR: advocacy and programme delivery were the two linked elements of a common strategy. With the objective of halving the infant and child deaths, he vividly used the spectre of 40,000 children dying each day and quickly unleashed an onslaught on the human conscience through the now widely available means of communications – both modern and traditional.

UNICEF's annual publication *The State of the World's Children Report* became a leading tool for advocacy, achieving worldwide outreach and often front page media coverage. JPG also mobilized the political establishments of both the developing and the industrialized world. He went to see heads of state and government, leaders both spiritual and temporal to plead the unconscionability of infants and children dying at such a rate when the means of averting these deaths were readily available at such a low cost. He felt that it was an injustice that the readily available, doable measures should not be taken. In making his visits, JPG always conducted demonstrations to back up his advocacy – foil packets of oral rehydration salts which could be used to replace the electrolytes lost in common diarrhoea, at a cost of less than ten cents per packet. He would explain that it generally required only about two packets to save a child's life. All of his advocacy for child survival carried a promise of UNICEF support. He was an effective mobilizer of presidents and ministers, of NGOs and religious groups, of village and community leaders, of parents and young people – and it bore fruit in a short time.

The second element in his dual strategy was to ensure that the countries which committed to UCI got appropriate support in programme delivery. The magnitude of the challenge was global and necessitated a global movement of both international and national partners, with UNICEF serving as a catalyst for support.

JPG is fondly remembered as a master strategist – the one who knew how to make things happen. He charted a course of action, helped to solve problems and cleared roadblocks. He introduced many new strategic elements and also changed emphases and methods in programme operations as the need arose.

While the child survival programmes had many traditional features, they also incorporated features unique in many ways.

Political will

Although it has been much talked about, very little has been written about political will and commitment. The child survival programmes consciously mobilized political will and commitment from both ends – top down from heads of state and government and bottom up from the people and communities. Political will enhanced the visibility of the programme while serving as a tool for advocacy and public mobilization. The involvement of heads of state and government and successive hierarchical levels enabled mobilization of the government machinery. It was also found that at sub-national levels, officials of the interior ministries and local government like governors, mayors, district chiefs down to village chiefs played a very important role in mobilizing the whole administrative structure as they are pivotal in local administration. Political will also ensures the flow of funds through budgetary allocations which ultimately contributed towards success and sustainability.

Experience indicates that political will is easier to establish when it is 'good politics' to do so. All political leaders want to be popular and linked to success. Programmes must be doable with results and measurable impact in the not too distant future. Political life spans are short in many developing countries, especially where instability persists. It is therefore easier to generate political will if leaders can expect results during their political lives in office which is generally about three to four years. It also helps when the programmes are low cost in nature, simple and understandable.

Social mobilization

Although the term and widespread adoption seemed new in the 1980s, the concept was not. Social mobilization entails mobilizing the society for a cause. Successful social mobilization efforts have several features in common. These include conscious generation and establishment of political will, widespread use of different types of communications and media, active community involvement and the participation of different sectors of the population. JPG helped mobilize support for child survival programmes in many countries using religious and civic leaders, artists and intellectuals, as well as professionals and government leaders. All this lent legitimacy to the child survival efforts.

Legitimation is an important element of social mobilization since it erases doubts and misapprehensions. It can be achieved internationally through the adoption of the goals and objectives by competent international bodies such as the World Health Assembly on health matters, by involvement of national and global leaders and statesmen, or through professional approval. The use of oral rehydration therapy (ORT), for example, was initially viewed with sceptism, when standard treatment involved the use of intravenous fluids. But after the medical profession had endorsed ORT, opinion shifted. JPG endlessly quoted the comments made in *The Lancet*, one of the world's leading medical journals. This discussed oral rehydration therapy as *'potentially the most important medical advance this century.'* It proved to be a powerful weapon in promoting acceptance of ORT.

Legitimation was also conferred by the endorsement of religious leaders. For example, during the promotion of breastfeeding in the Islamic countries, the edict of the world-renowned Al-Azher University of Egypt that the Prophet Mohammad had decreed that all mothers should breastfeed their children for two years dissolved all doubts in the communities of the faithful. Social mobilization activities were used to create a movement with a life of its own, leading to institutionalization and sustainability.

Programme communications

Programme communications was an essential element of all successful programmes since good communications provided visibility and helped to create understanding, easier acceptance and participation by the population. Mass media now meant it was possible to reach whole populations. Inexpensive cassette tapes and transistor radios were available throughout the developing world and were enriching the potential of a global communications revolution for information, education and entertainment. (It is interesting to note that humble cassettes with messages from Ayatollah Khomeni were the principal means of mobilization of the Iranian revolution.)

Since most of the people in developing countries, with the probable exception of Latin America, live in rural areas the means of traditional communications through plays, puppets, songs and dance continue to serve as the principal means of reaching especially the rural and poor segment of the population. Modern mass media, however, has played an increasingly important role in programme communications. Television is considered the most effective and mesmerizing medium. However, its effectiveness is limited by the availability of electricity, the still relatively expensive television sets and their outreach which is frequently confined only to urban centres. But wherever it is accessible, the television remains the most powerful form of mass media. The effectiveness of print media is limited because not all people are literate and there are no newspapers or magazines which reach or are read by the whole population. The print media, however, has one major advantage – it has a longer shelf life and it is read by all decision makers. The radio is still the most effective media for programmatic purposes because it now reaches the most remote parts of each country and is generally listened to as the principal source for news, information and entertainment.

An interesting experience during the UCI campaign was the extensive use of posters showing the heads of state or prime ministers immunizing children, usually giving polio drops orally. From a programmatic point of view, these posters were highly effective health education and mobilization materials. They portrayed the importance the national leaders gave to immunization activities and also ensured the active participation of the whole governmental machinery. When the vaccine was given to their own children or grandchildren, it also conveyed the message that these vaccines are effective and safe. And national leaders loved the posters, since they showed the more humane side of their leadership.

Management by objectives

UNICEF is a decentralized organization with field offices exercising a large degree of autonomy. As part of pursuing the child survival and development goals, management by objectives was introduced. After agreeing on the goals and targets and the operational norms to be observed, each field office was allowed flexibility of operations and course changes in response to the results of close monitoring. Managers began to utilize problem solving skills more effectively as accountability and motivation became more widespread. The headquarters and regional offices served as monitoring centres with guidance and support functions to assist field offices. While creative tensions occasionally occurred, programme operations on the whole went smoothly and produced impressive results.

Innovative approaches and adaptation

When achieving a common global goal becomes imperative, countries generate their own innovative approaches to solve problems and make adaptations to suit local conditions. For example Sierra Leone, a country with high illiteracy and poor records, developed a system of using inexpensive plastic bracelets for children to denote the shots they had received. Different colours denoted different antigens. This helped reduced the drop out rates. China, on the other hand introduced a vaccination insurance contract system, whereby the vaccinator agreed to give prescribed vaccinations on time for a fee and in return would pay all medical expenses and compensation if the child fell sick of the diseases from which they were supposed to be protected.

Alliance building

JPG was a strong believer in alliances. Alliances add strength to a movement. So, JPG always looked positively at the contribution which could be made by a person or an organization. He felt a movement like child survival needed to generate a consensus and a thrust to have the desired impact – and the impact would be greater if it were of a global and universal character.

The first global partnership was built with the World Health Organization, the World Bank, United Nations Development Programme (UNDP) and the Rockefeller Foundation. As an obvious natural partner for child health and survival, WHO welcomed UNICEF's active interest in immunization and other child survival activities. JPG always believed that the expertise of WHO in health and the strong operational capacity of UNICEF in the field would be mutually advantageous and complementary.

JPG had links with the Rockefeller Foundation since his father's days. The Rockefeller Foundation had long been known for its interest and heavy investment in public health in developing countries and was the premier foundation for international health. In the case of the World Bank, JPG sought a partnership partly for their direct support and also because their partnership would help provide balance to the stress on economic development. He also strongly believed that preparing people for work and development through improving their health, nutrition and education and fulfilling their basic needs was essential in development. Also, the participation of the World Bank would lend credence to the bilateral development agencies to support child health and survival. For the Bank, this involvement would provide an opportunity to participate in a good social and human development programme and humanize its image. The then President of the World Bank, Barber Conable, later called the partnership a *'Grand Alliance.'*

The participation of UNDP was especially useful because the UNDP resident representatives generally served as the resident coordinator of the United Nations System at the field level. This would also provide opportunities for UNDP to participate in this historic movement.

The core group, together with over 100 participants including 34 world leaders met in March 1984 at the Bellagio Conference Centre in Italy, at a conference sponsored by the Rockefeller Foundation. The conference met to consider how to better protect the health of the children. The meeting produced a plan not only to immunize all the world's children as an impetus to primary health care, but also to promote other effective means – ranging from oral rehydration to child spacing and family planning – where and when opportunities present themselves so as to reduce morbidity and mortality in the most vulnerable of all groups.

After the conference, the core group of five organizations was formed into the Task Force for Child Survival – a vehicle whose goal was to further the agreed upon Plan. Bill Foege, the former Director of the Centre for Disease Control and Prevention was appointed Executive Director of the Task Force. The Task Force served the useful and important function of providing a neutral forum to mobilize globally for child survival, with the focus on achieving UCI by 1990, learning from successes and exchanging experiences. It also provided opportunities for partner organizations to deliberate on policy and operational issues. As progress was made and the potential of achieving UCI became possible, the Task Force also provided the forum to map out plans beyond 1990.

Bellagio I was followed by Bellagio II at Cartagena in Colombia in October 1985, Bellagio III at Talloires in France in March 1988 and Bellagio IV in Bangkok, Thailand in March 1990. These Bellagio meetings were attended by ministers of health and senior representatives from developing countries, heads and technical experts from the five sponsoring agencies of the Task Force, senior representatives from bilateral agencies and non-governmental organizations, and representatives of the Task Force itself.

After Bellagio II, the meetings came to focus on analysis of the experiences of the immunization effort, in view of the markedly increasing activities and support for immunization to reach the goal of UCI by 1990. This engendered confidence and excitement that universal immunization of children would indeed become a reality.

With increasing confidence that the goal of UCI could be reached by 1990, Bellagio III began to address the broader goals to be achieved after 1990, as reflected in the Talloires Declaration. The Talloires goals were later refined in the Bangkok meeting. The Bangkok Affirmation was adopted in September 1990 at the World Summit for Children as the goals for children and development to be achieved by the year 2000.

The World Summit for Children was the culmination of a steady progress of alliance building. It showed the political foresight of JPG and later served as a model in organizing other summits in the last decade of the century.

JPG's alliance building was not only at the global level, but also at the bilateral and non-governmental level. He felt that while global alliances were necessary, effective partnerships at the country level would have to include bilateral development agencies whose support were strongest at the country level. His work with two agencies may suffice to show his approach.

JPG felt his own government, the United States, should set an example. JPG worked feverishly with other lobbyists for an earmarking for child survival. The Congress established the Child Survival Fund in 1985 with an initial allocation of $25 million (it is now over $500 million) to be shared between USAID and UNICEF. Congress was willing to allocate the total amount to UNICEF, but JPG wished and urged that it be shared with USAID. Since UNICEF was always short on money, we asked him why he did not accept all the money. JPG agreed with the argument about our need for funds, but made a profound statement which illustrated his sense of strategic thinking. With this congressional allocation, he said, USAID would become a full partner in child survival, spending not only the funds earmarked for the purpose but other funds also. Later events, of course, proved this to be true.

JPG also kept a sharp eye on developments abroad. Hearing of the debate in the Italian Parliament and complaints about the existing programmes of development assistance, he realized Italian authorities would soon be looking for new ideas and proposals. He went to Italy with a specific and practical proposal for $100 million to finance the immunization efforts in Africa, a region of special interest for Italy. Italy agreed and their support came at a time when the funds were running short due to the rapid expansion of UCI activities.

In the non-government sector, JPG's outstanding success was his ability to mobilize Rotary International for all the vaccines needed to eradicate poliomyelitis. Rotary International pledged to raise $130 million but by early 1990 they had already raised $240 million. Equally important, Rotary International mobilized their members to help with national immunization days in hundreds of cities around the world.

Competition and emulation

To learn from one another and succeed has always been a stimulating experience, and UCI was no exception. However, to learn from success, there must be successful experiences. If they do not already exist, they must be created, nurtured and supported. This required seeking countries with viable experience, committed leadership, effective organization and broad participation. Colombia under President Betancur became the first country to show the way. Latin America had adopted the National Immunization Days approach to enable complete coverage for polio vaccination. In Colombia, a major mobilization of all sectors of the society took place, including the military and the Church. The military ensured the availability of vaccines in remote areas while, during baptisms and weddings, the priests in Catholic churches began to advise new parents and newly weds of the need to immunize their children. It was a vivid example of social mobilization with the involvement of the governmental structures led by the President, supported by the full force of communications and the participation of the media, artists and intellectuals, enthusiastic participation of the people and non-governmental organizations, and a prominent role played by the church.

Colombia was soon followed in 1984 by Burkina Faso under the youthful President Thomas Sankara and Turkey in 1985 under Prime Minister Turgut Ozal, an old colleague of JPG from the Green Revolution days. Visits especially to Colombia in the early days were made by delegations from other countries to discuss and evaluate their experiences. I recall seeing the Secretary of Health of Bangladesh in New York on his return from Colombia. I still remember his answer when I asked him for his impressions of the visit. Although the immunization coverage of Bangladesh at the time was in the range of 20 to 30 per cent, he confidently assured me that they would beat Colombia in two to three years. He said he would change and do some of the activities differently. True to his word, Bangladesh made unbelievable strides. The exchange of experience was broadened and countries learned from one another. But more importantly, a process of competition also emerged, each country trying to outdo the other. The process of a healthy competition was now underway.

This experience was later refined by the Philippines which produced coloured maps of different provinces and cities showing the different status of coverage of the different goals – setting up a process of competition and remedial action for areas which were less advanced.

Going to scale

It was the firm belief of JPG that if any interventions were to be effective and lasting, they would have to go to scale, covering the whole country or at least a sizable portion of the population. When an intervention is of a limited scale, it is more likely that the poorest and most disadvantaged population will be bypassed and ignored because they are generally more difficult to reach and have less political clout. Projects of limited scope are also less likely to be sustained and institutionalized because the costs are generally higher and the involvement of foreign expertise is stronger. These are deterrents to replication.

The delivery of social services can, of course, be extended nationwide by incremental increases through state or private delivery channels, if the costs can be absorbed. The process, however, takes a long time and the cumulative results may not be visible for years unless there is a strong popular demand to which the government is responsive. This option is thus more limited to countries which can afford its implications in terms of cost and time.

The rational alternative for most developing countries in extending services nationwide over a relatively short period of time requires more than traditional progressive quantitative change. A qualitative change is needed leading to popular internalization of programme objectives. A double dynamic is set in motion. When all sectors of the population have accepted the programme objectives as a national goal, human resources can be mobilized from all walks of life on a voluntary basis. Simultaneously, felt needs are transformed into a firm popular demand and a self-sustaining momentum is then achieved. These programme objectives must however be achievable through a course of actions that is effective and affordable. The degree of success is, however, dependent on the visibility of benefits, the simplicity of ideas and of actions and their manageability, a conducive atmosphere and the ripeness of situation and timing, broad participation and good efficient organization.

Going to scale is thus essentially a process of education, motivation and mobilization.

JPG had personal experience of going to scale through his involvement in the Turkish Green Revolution during the 1960s, mobilizing peasant farmers to adopt the new seeds and going from a few hundred farmers to thousands in two or three years. He now had the opportunity of successfully applying it to a social sector initiative.

Status of Achievements

When the objective of reaching universal child immunization was set, the criteria of 'universality' was not clearly defined. Two issues of universality were hotly debated by the participants. These two issues were, firstly, how to calculate the immunization coverage and, secondly, what percentage of immunization would constitute UCI.

A concept generally used in immunization was to count the fully immunized child – meaning the child who has received all six antigens. This required eight shots (one BCG, three DPT, three OPV and one measles). While theoretically it seemed logical, operationally it meant that a child would not be counted unless he or she had received all the eight shots. Even if a child had received seven shots, providing protection against three groups of diseases, the child would still not be counted. Similarly when universality was defined, purists wanted to establish it as covering 100 per cent of the child population. But even in industrialized countries, with transportation readily available, all urban and rural areas accessible, and awareness higher, the coverage rarely reached 100 per cent at age one.

The third element of coverage required to reach consensus was the age range. As measles shots were given much later in the industrialized countries, it was discussed whether the same time table should be followed in the developing countries. But in developing countries, measles is a principal killer of children and the onslaught of the disease occurs much earlier, generally before age one. It was therefore agreed that efforts should be made to reach children before one year of age and that only those receiving their measles immunization under one would be counted for the statistics on coverage.

The genius of JPG was pragmatism, in the best and broadest sense of the word. In addition to the above arguments, he emphasized the need for definitions which would help mobilize action. He pointed out that countries should not be set up for failure by fixing standards so high that no country could reach them despite their best efforts. This led to heated debate but eventually the consensus was reached that immunization coverage would be reported based on the coverage of each of the six antigens (in the case of DPT and OPV, only the third dose). The basic national coverage required to qualify as 'universal' would be set at 80 per cent. Eighty per cent is a useful target as it is high enough to need special effort and acceleration but not so high as to be out of reach. It was also thought that such a high percentage might also provide a degree of herd immunity.

Although the global target was set at 80 per cent coverage for each antigen, African health ministers later set the target for the continent at 75 per cent because of its lower initial base and many unstable conditions prevailing at the time. China, on the other hand, set the target higher at 85 per cent.

Thus defined, the number of developing countries achieving UCI in all antigens increased year by year. In 1986, sixteen countries reached UCI, followed by 34 in 1988, 43 in 1989 and 64 at the end of 1990. By the end of 1990 the global target of 80 per cent of the infant population under one year of age was achieved on average in the developing world for each of the six antigens.

The success of this effort served to reduce mortality from vaccine-preventable diseases by an estimated three million and meant a reduction of over 400,000 paralytic polio cases in 1990 alone. This was the outcome of a monumental effort by the whole world on behalf of children. This achievement was a tremendous success and was widely praised. JPG often referred to UCI efforts as the largest peacetime mobilization in history.

Building on momentum and success

The 1980s was a lost decade for development. It was a decade of despair for most of the developing world except for East and Southeast Asia, with severe cutbacks in the social sector. In Africa, there was a collapse of infrastructure, health care and school systems; health centres were without drugs and health workers and teachers were not paid, or paid several months late, with the result that the systems were fast becoming dysfunctional. Schools were without books and preventive health care was severely curtailed. These were dark times indeed.

Yet the child survival efforts made it a decade of new hope. It saw the birth of the Child Survival and Development Revolution with emphasis on preventive health based on effective low cost technology. It witnessed the generation of political will and commitment, social mobilization and effective use of the communications revolution for children on a global scale.

The CSDR exhibited true multi-sectorality, went to scale, set goals and targets, introduced management by objectives and delivered results.

The end of the decade saw several unique advancements for children which became possible because UCI was achieved. The achievement of UCI gave the world confidence to move forward and to convene the World Summit for Children, to hold the World Conference on Education for All and to adopt the Convention on the Rights of the Child. All these achievements would not have been possible without the vision, leadership and contributions of James P. Grant.

Convention on the Rights of the Child

The Convention on the Rights of the Child was adopted by the United Nations General Assembly on 20 November 1989 and came into force on 2 September 1990. Although Professor Lapotka of Poland and Nils Thedin, the President of the Swedish National Committee for UNICEF deserve full credit for their untiring efforts to initiate, promote and advance the idea, it would also be wrong to say that it would have reached where it has without the active support and mobilization of JPG.

When the Convention was first conceptualized, it focused mainly on protection of the child. JPG felt protection alone was too narrow and would be difficult to operationalize. He suggested the inclusion of 'survival' and 'development' rights so that it would be more inclusive and would bring governments into the overall context of implementing the Convention. He also wanted to be able to use the Convention once it came into force as a moral force to advance the well-being of children on all three fronts: survival, protection and development.

The Bamako Initiative

With UCI making good progress in the late 1980s, JPG began to explore two further challenges. How could UCI and other achievements be sustained, especially in countries which had suffered from the severe effects of economic recession and adjustment measures, and how could the scope of the Child Survival and Development Revolution be broadened and consolidated?

The recession had its most severe impact in Africa where health structures were collapsing especially through lack of drugs and non-payment of salaries to health workers. The breakthrough came to JPG in September 1987 when he was attending the WHO Regional Committee for Africa, whose membership comprised the health ministers of Africa. Together with Hafdan Mahler, the then Director-General of WHO who was also attending the meeting, they submitted a joint WHO/UNICEF proposal which later came to be known as the 'Bamako Initiative'.

Under this initiative, the principle of community financing of health care was proposed, based on the successful experience of the Pahou project in Benin. An initial two-year supply of essential drugs was to be provided by UNICEF to the health centres and the drugs would be sold to the community with a mark up. Even with a mark up sufficient to cover the replacement cost of the drugs and the costs of community health workers, the drugs would still be cheaper than the market price. In some countries, charges were not on drugs used, but on clinic visits. The drugs would be replenished with the money collected and the profits used for payment of honoraria to health workers and for other incidental expenses of the centre.

It was found that communities were willing to pay if services were improved. Different forms of payment were tried and the problem of exemption of payment for the very poor remained a challenge. The issue was how to identify the poor. The common practice was to leave it to the community concerned to define and identify its own poor. It is noteworthy that the insurance system which was tried out in one country did not work because the young and healthy would not join as their need for the service was less. In most of the Bamako Initiative projects, little leakage was found. Receipt and sale of drugs were properly recorded, money collected was managed by committee and deposited in the bank or post office savings accounts.

The 1992 evaluation of the Bamako Initiative by the London School of Hygiene and Tropical Medicine states : *'The overall conclusion is that much looks promising. UNICEF and other agencies should continue to support countries' efforts to implement the Bamako Initiative and the need for substantial investment in the process should be recognized.'*

JPG believed that the sustainability of UCI would have to be in the context of health systems and structures and properly functioning systems thus became imperative.

World Summit for Children

With the achievement of UCI imminent, JPG took two steps to consolidate and broaden the scope of the Child Survival and Development Revolution.

He worked at the professional level to explore new goals for children and women which were scientifically sound and operationally doable and achievable, and he also worked towards a global political commitment to further the broader goals for children and women to be achieved before the end of the century.

He entrusted the task of framing the new goals to the Task Force for Child Survival. As earlier described, these were developed, discussed and endorsed at the Bellagio III meeting in Talloires, France in 1988 as the Declaration of Talloires and at the Bellagio IV meeting in Bangkok as the Affirmation of Bangkok. These goals were later officially endorsed by the World Health Assembly and the World Conference on Education for All.

In order to mobilize global political commitment, JPG envisaged a World Summit for Children in the latter part of 1990 when news of successes like UCI would be more evident and consolidation of success would be explored. However, he did not want the Summit to be another United Nations meeting but a conference sponsored by the national governments for fellow governments. Thus, JPG worked closely with the governments of Canada, Egypt, Mali, Mexico, Pakistan and Sweden who became the six 'initiator countries' of the Summit.

The World Summit for Children was held in the United Nations premises in New York on 30 September 1990, attended by 71 heads of state or government and 88 other plenipotentiaries. It issued a World Declaration and a Plan of Action for the Survival, Protection and Development of Children in the 1990's.

The Declaration established the principle of 'First Call for Children' and committed the participants to a 10-point programme to protect the rights of children and to improve their lives. The Plan of Action described the specific actions for child survival, protection and development in the 1990s. The Summit also asked each country to prepare a National Plan of Action and entrusted the United Nations to institute appropriate mechanisms for monitoring the implementation of the Plan of Action and to arrange for a mid-decade review in 1995. The Summit goals were eventually endorsed by over 150 heads of state or government.

Mid-Decade Goals

By 1993 the Plan of Action had given rise to the development and adoption of National Plans of Action in about 150 countries, covering over 90 per cent of the world's population. The first three years after the Summit also saw a series of regional meetings reaffirming the Summit commitments and exchanging information and experience on their plans to reach the end-decade goals.

Regional meetings in Dhaka, Bangladesh and Dakar, Senegal gave rise to the concept of mid-decade goals – a set of goals delineated for achievement by 1995. The 'Mid-Decade Goals' were later endorsed by other regions. JPG used to refer to these goals as stepping stone goals, constituting a low-cost, high impact set of tasks to help set the stage for attainment of the Summit goals for the year 2000. These goals were premised on the fact that political will is easier to establish when goals are more 'doable' and manageable and also the need for intermediate stages to build up momentum. It was also believed that success would breed success and would provide confidence to deal with bigger challenges.

In 1994, the last full year of JPG's stewardship, many countries were working seriously towards the achievement of mid-decade goals. JPG made an assessment that, by 1995, the majority of the countries would be achieving the majority of the goals. He saw the adoption of the Bamako Initiative in all west and central African countries and in some east African countries with the emergence of new opportunities to influence sector reforms and systems building. Seventy eight per cent of UCI countries had sustained or increased their immunization coverage in measles and 79 per cent had done so in DPT3. In non-UCI countries, 82 per cent had increased or sustained their coverage in measles and 77 per cent in DPT3. Polio had been wiped out in 145 countries and 84 countries had already seem a 90 per cent reduction in measles incidence.

The ORT use, Universal Salt Iodization and Vitamin A deficiency control were making good progress. The ORT use in 1994 was 57 per cent compared to 17 per cent in 1985 with some notable achievements such as Bangladesh where usage was at 91 per cent. Wherever ORT posts were functioning, no watery diarrhoea deaths were reported any more.

Universal Salt Iodization (USI) was the strongest movement since UCI. It captured the imagination of national leaders and countries. JPG carried a small starch solution bottle and tested whether the salt at meetings and even at the presidential dining tables was iodized. By 1994, about 75 to 80 per cent of salt was iodized and the target was set at 95 per cent by 1996.

The reduction of Vitamin A deficiency was another goal receiving close attention through diet diversification, supplementation and fortification.

Fortification of food was emerging as the most sustainable route learning from the success of the fortification of sugar in Guatemala at a cost of 17 cents per capita per year.

A tribute

Working in UNICEF during the last ten years of JPG's tenure has been a most exhilarating and rewarding experience for many staff members. With high adrenaline, we all tried to scale heights previously thought impossible, making dreams come true. Starting with CSDR, achieving UCI and moving on to decade and mid-decade goals on a global scale, the experience was unrivalled.

In chemical laboratories, a combination of hydrogen gas and oxygen gas will only produce a mixture of two gases. To transform them into water, a qualitative change is needed through an electric spark. Similarly, a spark to ignite the movement is inspiring leadership. Inspiring leadership stimulates participation, motivation and innovation to surmount difficulties and roadblocks and ultimately leads to success and sustaining the achievements. Jim Grant was a genius – a giant of a man. This essay covers only one aspect of his contributions, and that only inadequately. He had a rare mix of vision and effective leadership, with a strategic mind which always seemed to know how to reach the goals and targets he had set. He knew how to turn dreams into reality. He was a leader who could inspire and lead his troops and help them achieve their goals. He had a positive outlook which always looked at the bright side of events and a generosity which always showed him ready to share his achievements and successes. It was a pleasure and an honour to work for him and to work with him. It was like watching a shooting star – a shining path of light which illuminates the world, but alas, it was no more.

Dancing with a villager during a campaign in China

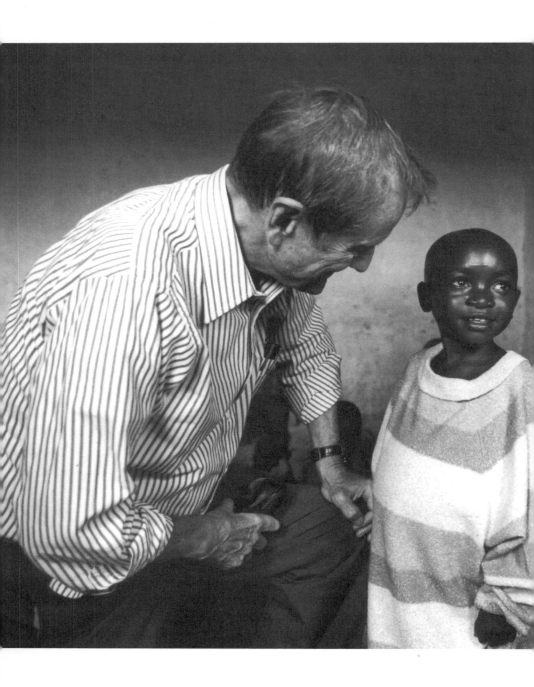

Stopping wars for children

by Richard Reid

It wasn't Jim Grant who invented the idea of stopping wars to reach and protect children. Nils Thedin, for many years the head of the Swedish National Committee for UNICEF, did that – and he persisted in pushing his idea of 'children as a zone of peace' when few would listen. But it was Jim who in time saw the beauty of Thedin's idea and made it operational.

A 'zone' was a conceptual place. Children were scattered everywhere in countries at war. But a period of time – a 'period of tranquility' – was something that Jim Grant thought might be concrete and sustainable. If a forceful demand for a period of child protection could be laid out persuasively, in comprehensive terms, to the antagonists in a conflict area, it might lead to more than calling a halt in the shooting to reach children. It could also be a dramatic demonstration of the potential force of the Convention on the Rights of the Child. And it could be an opening wedge for broader humanitarian interventions in war.

Jim Grant applied the idea of military stand-downs for children in the wars in El Salvador in 1985, Lebanon in 1987, Sudan in 1989 and Iraq in 1991. The conflicts in each place were halted for 'periods of tranquility' – ranging in length from several hours to months. Each was a high-risk juggling act. Each produced remarkable, sometimes spectacular results that were documented. None would have worked without the steady hand and personal magic of Jim Grant.

This is an account of his leadership in those efforts.

Sudan

Was Jim Grant like other people? Those of us who knew him would have laughed out loud at the suggestion. He had the energy of a particle accelerator. He thrived on stress; it seemed to nourish him. The same was true for marathon working hours and the burdens of responsibility – OK, add more weight, I'm ready, he seemed to say.

Whatever the big picture was, Jim could see it whole, nuances and operational details, start to finish, usually before others had even begun to imagine it. He woke up in the morning in his airplane seat, beaming, because he already had in his head a fast-forward film of exactly how the day, and the days to follow, would unfold – along with a fall-back plan or two in case they unfolded differently.

Did he ever tire or lose his cheer? Not on my watch. He led by robust example – which is to say that he drew others along with him at flank speed as he half-jogged across desert terrain, worked his way through refugee camps with spindly three-year-olds in his arms, drafted telexes in jeeps, and sat up until three in the morning coaxing agreements out of prime ministers. At six the same morning he would be out of bed, jabbing a pencil at a map over breakfast, laughing and insisting, *'It's doable. It's doable!'*

For all the sunshine he brought, though, Jim also wanted results. There was a twinkle in his eye; behind it there was a glint. Trying to tell him *'no'* was as hopeless as wrestling with an angel. You knew he would finally prevail.

Yet Jim Grant almost never showed impatience. He never fumed when things went wrong – even big things. Usually he was there with another strategy as good as the original, but if not, he was philosophical. He listened, he understood, he forgave.

I only saw Jim Grant angry once. It was on a hot evening in April 1989, in Khartoum, Sudan. The UN agencies, led by UNICEF, were at the break point of an effort to use a three month ceasefire in the Sudanese civil war, a 'Period of Tranquility', to make the country's single train line run before the rainy season started. Jim himself had engineered the ceasefire by bringing around Prime Minister Sadiq el Mahdi and John Garang, the leader of the rebel Sudan People's Liberation Army. To pump up international pressure on them, he had pulled political stops from Washington to Moscow to Addis Ababa. One hundred and ten thousand tons of food grain had to reach the south quickly if Operation Lifeline Sudan, the multi-agency UN effort Jim was leading, was to stave off an estimated half million deaths by famine and disease – deaths mainly of young children and women. Of course the cargo planes that Jim and the donors had assembled were important, and so were the truck routes and barges on the newly opened Nile, but without the train and its delivery capacity, Operation Lifeline Sudan would fizzle.

All of this was chancy. It had taken a full-scale resurrection to get the train line between Muglad and Aweil running. For the better part of ten years, some said more, nothing had rolled down those narrow-gauge rails. The war had made the line too dangerous. It ran through the territory of bandit militias. Where sand or grass hadn't covered the rails, whole sections of track had sprung. Ties had been stolen. To clear the way and cobble the tracks back together again, the government was dragooning hundreds of laborers from Khartoum. They were mainly Muslim Arabs with little sympathy for the rebel Christians in the South. And there were all-night negotiations with the trainmen's union to fix wages and figure out a risk-indemnity scale.

So the meeting among the 20-odd people in the conference room in Khartoum that evening was one of tense expectation. In the city, anyone who read or watched TV was talking about American and European news bulletins on the ceasefire – and the train. The Sudan story had become a global item.

Around the table were government ministers and Relief and Rehabilitation Committee officials, donor ambassadors, NGO representatives, UN agency people of different ranks, and two of us from UNICEF besides Jim Grant. All had come to be briefed by Jim on how the train's morning trial run out of Muglad had gone. Some, though, were murmuring about rumors that the train had been shot up and boarded.

One of the government ministers looked uncomfortable. He was an army general from a prominent family, who was known to head a clan that controlled a large militia operating south of Muglad. He had pledged to Jim that his people would leave the train alone. Apparently things had turned out differently.

Jim began to speak, measuring his syllables. I saw a flush on his cheeks. He looked straight at the general, and then at each of the people in the room.

'We've been let down,' he said. *'Someone has let us down.'*

Dead silence.

'There was an attack on the train this morning by an armed militia.' People rustled in their seats but no one spoke. *'Three members of the train crew were*

shot. They're in the hospital, expected to live. Some of the freight cars were badly damaged – probably too damaged to use again. I wonder how this happened?'

He waited. No one spoke.

'We're here to save lives. Not endanger them. All of us. Isn't that right?' He almost shouted the words.

'It will take all of us,' he said, *'All of us in this room. We've come too far to be tripped up now. The UN Secretary General has charged me with making this operation work. I plan do to that.'*

He looked around the room at everyone again, slowly, one by one, and last at the general. *'With your help.'* He pronounced each of the three words separately. Everyone looked away from the general.

'If you know anyone else who wants to try to stop this train, tell them hands off. Hands off! Or we'll shine the headlights of the world on them.'

Jim sat back.

'I don't have anything else, Mr. Chairman. The train will do another trial run the day after tomorrow. The engineers and crew say they're ready. With your permission, we'll meet again that evening.'

A week later, after the train had made a maiden run to Aweil and unloaded with no mishaps, Jim drank kharkade with the general who headed the militia clan, and his wife, at an outdoor restaurant next to the Nile. Then they had dinner. The tables were packed together and full, but the place was quieter than usual.

Jim was telling stories – about children's vaccines crossing icy mountain streams in Turkey on the backs of donkeys, and government doctors being peaceably abducted during the El Salvador ceasefire to vaccinate kids on the rebel side of the lines. Heads were turning his way, lighting up with smiles.

'Can you imagine that?' the general shouted. *'Can you imagine?'*

The next day Jim flew back to New York. The general became one of the government's big supporters of Operation Lifeline Sudan. At a meeting two weeks or so later, sitting next to me, he turned and said, out of the blue, *'Mr. Grant is a great man. Yes. A great man.'*

Negotiations: the Government

It was easy enough to imagine that Sadiq el Mahdi was the great-great grandson of the Mahdi who had once swept across the desert and taken the measure of Chinese Gordon a few miles from where we sat waiting. His robe rippled as he crossed the hall in four-foot strides. He has a dark face, a nose like a scythe, and startling white teeth. He dressed in white from his burnoose to his slippers. He filled the room.

It was early March, 1989, at the Prime Minister's in Khartoum.

'Ah, Mr. Grant! We have met. You are welcome. Yes.'

As a student, Sadiq el Mahdi had headed the Oxford Union.

'Mr. Prime Minster, we are honoured to have your time.'

'You may have as much of it as you wish. Rather, I should say as much as you can endure. Which is what my ministers no doubt think, but never say. Yes.'

'That is kind of you, Excellency. I am sure your ministers are too loyal and busy to have such thoughts... I bring you the warm good wishes of the Secretary General. He has charged me with getting to the root of a humanitarian problem that afflicts many countries today. Countries troubled by civil conflict. Sudan especially, because of its size and challenges. And I would ask your good help in addressing this problem. If it can be done here, it can be done anywhere.'

'That is intriguing, Mr. Grant. 'It?' Do you mean the war? This war is imposed on us by false leaders and ideological bandits who say they want independence. This is a sovereign, unitary state. If they attack us and threaten the state, we have to respond. And crush the revolt. As we are doing. That has a simple logic.'

Jim nodded.

'Once that is done, we can stop fighting. I know that is what you want, Mr. Grant. To save the children. Admirable. I too want that.'

'I know that, Mr. Prime Minister.'

'They are slaughtering thousands.'

'Yes. Thousands may have fallen in combat, Mr. Prime Minister. I fear for a larger number – four million. They are not soldiers. Children. If the war goes on to the start of the rains, a quarter of a million will be dead by the end of August. Another half million will be hit so hard by hunger and disease that they will be impaired as long as they live.'

'No, no, not that many. That cannot be true. That's worse than Ethiopia.'

'It is worse than Ethiopia, Mr. Prime Minister. It was worse with the drought and the fighting in the south two years ago, and it will still be worse this year. The signs are there.'

'No one has shown them to me.' For a moment the Prime Minister's composure hardened. *'Take these facts to the rebels, Mr. Grant. They will just look at you. They buzz like gnats. They want a Dinka state.'*

'With your permission, I will talk to them.'

'You have it. Go to Ethiopia if you want. They are in a little town called Nazret. See the rebels.'

'With your permission, sir. Your written permission as the head of this government.'

'You will have it, or my final spoken word, this week. What would the United Nations expect to get from them?'

'An agreement to stop attacking long enough for us to get to the people before the rains, and prevent all those deaths. Prevent a humanitarian disaster that will make the world shudder.'

'Well, now, they will never stop until we mop them up. They're a loose gang of bandit opportunists who can't even agree on siege strategy. Look at Wau! But let's say they agree. What will you have?'

'Maybe half a solution, Mr. Prime Minister.'

'The other half?'

'Is for you and your army to do the same thing. With the rains, everything will be stuck fast. But at least the soldiers – on both sides – will have food and supplies to sit it out. Not the civilians who are fleeing from both sides. Not the little children.'

'Go see them, Mr. Grant. I say it: everyone in this room has now heard it. See them.'

He leaned forward with both fists before him on the table.

'But this is your initiative, a United Nations gesture, not to be construed as recognition of any kind... I do not like it. We permit it as a humanitarian shot in the dark. Not this government's position.'

'Of course I understand, Excellency. This undertaking comes from us, not the Government of Sudan. But let us take a hypothesis. Let us suppose that they agree. That the agreement from their side is as ironclad as battlefield agreements can be made. How might your government respond?'

'I enjoy your company, but I dislike this topic, Mr. Grant. Go see them. We will see. We will see. You will join me at dinner tonight?'

'Yes, Sir. Inshallah. Thank you.'

Jim Grant laid it all out before Sadiq el Mahdi that night at dinner. Within a month he, the Prime Minister, would host and chair in Khartoum a major international conference on the Sudan humanitarian emergency. The meeting would draw donor country ambassadors, heads of UN agencies, main NGOs, and the media. It would create and launch a coordinated multi-agency, multinational relief effort called Operation Lifeline Sudan. Before May, tons of food, medicine, seeds, animal vaccines, and fishnets, the staples of life, would stream into the south with the Prime Minister's blessing, and his government would join in monitoring the flow.

It took the Prime Minister a few weeks of wrangling with military and fundamentalist elements to squeeze out of his government a willingness to look at the UN relief plan – and a possible ceasefire. In the meantime, this writer went to a golf course in Addis Ababa for a clandestine meeting with an SPLA man on how and where Jim Grant could meet the rebel leadership – and John Garang.

Negotiations: the rebels

Kongor was a scattering of flimsy houses on the escarpments and dry savannah of south-central Sudan, somewhere between Pibor Post and Rumbek, far from the train line, set on a ruined, seldom used road. The Red Cross had made a base there, with a clinic that served a catchment area almost the size of Junglei Province. People would trek for days to come in for shots and treatment.

Jim Grant had come to Kongor by Cessna and jeep to meet with John Garang, the rebel leader, and a group of rebel field commanders. It was a baking hot day in the third week of April 1989. Three of us from UNICEF had come with Jim. The SPLA was in a triumphalist frame of mind. Step by step, they had taken all of the southern half of the country except for the army garrison towns and their perimeters. Now that they were on a roll, it would be hard to talk them into laying down their arms for three months. For us there were urgent humanitarian reasons, but would they buy?

A tall, solemn Garang, standing with his generals behind him, received us under a mango tree. He seldom came this far into Sudan except covertly, and when he did, he stayed on the move; his headquarters base was 600 miles east, in Ethiopia. He opened his arms and motioned to Jim to sit down on a stool across from him at the base of the tree. We followed. There were introductions and an exchange of compliments. Garang's voice was a mix of African/English and flat mid-western

American that he must have brought back from his university work in Iowa. Jim began without preamble.

'Dr. Garang, I'll be in London tomorrow, facing some hard questions from the media about the refugee and hunger situation here in your country, and I need your help in getting ready for them.'

'We'll give whatever help we can, Mr. Grant. I wonder if you have asked Sadiq and his people for their help.'

'Yes, I have, and I think we'll get it.'

A polite smile.

'You think. What have you asked them?'

'To stop fighting in May for three months.'

'May I ask what it is you want from us?'

'The same thing.'

'Well.' His eyebrows went up.

'In London tomorrow, what will you tell them?'

'What the Prime Minister has told me, and anything you may authorize me to say from your side.'

'Hold on, Mr. Grant. We are winning this war. You can see that. Before long we'll have Juba.'

'Why should you stop?'

'Yes. Why should we?' His commanders were whispering among themselves.

'In good sense any war should stop. All wars should stop. But the UN isn't asking you precisely that, Mr. Garang.'

'Then what?'

'A break in the fighting. Enough time for us to properly move in food and supplies. A period of tranquility. It's been done for the sake of children in El Salvador and Lebanon.'

'Why?'

'Dr. Garang, I know you're not just a resistance movement leader. You're a family man.' Jim smiled broadly and looked him in the eye.

'Can I ask how many children you have?'

Garang's commanders laughed and covered their mouths. Jim went on.

'You have four million!'

Loud laughter erupted. Garang chuckled and studied Jim. He shrugged and spread his hands.

'Am I such a mighty man?'

'Well, if you look at it, you'll see you are. No one in the south has more real power, more control – or more ability to make things happen. In an important way, doesn't that make you the father of all the children here?'

'Well .'

'There are about four million, if you count the babies up to the 12 year-olds. And most of them are in a bad way that will become critical once the rains come.'

'Do we take on that responsibility, Mr. Grant? We are an army.'

'Maybe that's all you were once,' Jim said. 'But now you're the de facto government. Your commanders here are like district commissioners. Governors. I hear about schools and well-clearing.'

'Yes?'

'And so you are already acting like the father of the poor and needy in the south. It falls to the leader to be the protector. It goes beyond fighting a war. Sometimes opportunity can take leadership to another level. I think those four million children are an opportunity.'

'I'm not sure you people in the United Nations understand our big opportunity now, Mr. Grant. Our fight is on the upswing. We have a chance for freedom. For autonomy. Look at this map.' A commander passed him a map that he showed to Jim, who studied it and looked up.

'After the rains, will your chances be any less? Won't both sides be immobilized before long, anyway? Isn't it time to show the world something besides rotting bodies in the desert?' Jim leaned forward. He spoke quietly.

'If your forces stand down, starting the week after next, and the government troops do the same, we can start moving that food grain without danger. And it will be on the historical record that you chose humanitarian principle over military advantage.'

'Military victory, Mr. Grant.'

'I believe you're disposed to this kind of humane effort, Dr. Garang. You've set up your own relief group. We can supply it, lend you people, help you build it up.'

Garang stood up, excused himself, and walked a distance into the bright sunshine with his commanders.

They were back in ten minutes. Garang sat on his stool and looked at Jim without speaking.

'Can I tell the Prime Minister that you are ready for a military stand down from the end of next month?' Jim waited.

'I have great doubts. We are a decentralized movement. Our forces are scattered.'

'I speak to you today as the leader of a people. As I have spoken to other leaders around the world.'

'You make things hard, Mr. Grant.'

'No, Dr. Garang. You chose a hard life, and you are bearing it and sometimes smiling. This hard act will lift your heart. When can I hear from you?'

Garang winced and shook his head. For several minutes he turned away to speak to his commanders in Dinka.

'Saturday, Sir. Mr. Lam Akol here will bring you our decision. I make no promises.'

'Saturday it is. I will tell the Prime Minister the question is open until then. We will count on this. Four million children.'

They shook hands.

'You are a hard man, Mr. Grant. I believe you want to do the right thing.'

'Thank you. I play a weak hand except when you consider the children.'

On Saturday we received word through SPLA sources in Addis Ababa and by radio in Khartoum that the rebels would observe a three month period of tranquility. Lying open to us now, cleared of ambushes and roadblocks for the first time, was an area the size of France and Germany. And if there weren't four million children in it, there were fully three. Jim Grant had his work cut out for him.

It had to be short work, because time was running out. Jim won agreement from the Khartoum government for a radical addition to the food delivery plan – a cross-border scheme that would see trucks bring food up into the south of Sudan from a UN storage base to be set up at Lokichokio in Northwest Kenya. Operation Lifeline Sudan began to take on a life of its own. By mid-May, with the rains not far off, thousands of people had hands on involvement in the operation: the Khartoum bureaucracy, the increasingly large UN field staff, UN guards and volunteers for the barge and train routes, SPLA soldiers and non-military administrators, large and small NGOs, and the Red Cross in vital parallel actions. The Sudanese army and the SPLA had backed away from the supply routes, except to join in clearance and secondary transport deliveries.

There were setbacks and human costs. I saw Jim choke up as he passed among the beds at the Red Cross field hospital in Lokichokio, where several Kenyan UN drivers lay with burns and bullet wounds from a road ambush by a raider tribe. But the corridors of tranquility held for the three months Jim had planned. Operation Lifeline Sudan did stave off disaster. The 110,000 tons of food were delivered, unevenly but sufficiently, and there was no famine. Child deaths for the year beginning in May 1989 were not measurably higher than in non-emergency years.

Just as important for Jim Grant was the precedent Operation Lifeline Sudan established: the humanitarian imperative to separate the sides, even in a major war with extended battle lines, long enough to protect vulnerable populations. Like Archimedes with his fulcrum, Jim leveraged this precedent often afterward, in places as diverse as Ethiopia , Angola, Iraq, and the former Yugoslavia. And he made sure it was enshrined in the 1990 Declaration of the World Summit for Children, which urged that *'periods of tranquility and special relief corridors be observed for the benefit of children, where war and violence... are taking,place.'* More than 150 heads of state or government signed that Declaration.

After Operation Lifeline Sudan, I began to see that when Jim Grant went into war zones and negotiated these periods of tranquility to save children, he might be up to something larger. He was up to peace, wasn't he? War by war, he was refining the formula.

Lebanon

Sudan's was a low-intensity war, spread over thousands of miles, a chronic infection that had sapped the country for eight years. Lebanon's was more like epilepsy – a kind of armed communal epilepsy, chronic for more than a decade and much more immediately violent than Sudan. Six factions in a time warp, blasting each other at close quarters in a small, urbanized country.

Jim Grant knew the country. He had visited Beirut and gone up and down the coast more than once in the early 1980s. Now, in the summer of 1987, Jim was focusing on Lebanon with a special intent. Lebanon was the conspicuous laggard in an Arab region that was leading the world in child immunization percentages. It had dropped off the tables. Universal child immunization was the keystone goal of the Child Survival Revolution. Jim Grant was determined that his global team would meet that goal – everywhere.

In Lebanon Jim clearly saw the trophy aspect – the demonstration value. The days of tranquility in El Salvador in 1985 had had a powerful knock on effect across Central America. It was time to show again, in another region familiar with war, that the impossible wasn't far fetched. Incentives were the fuel of Jim Grant's advocacy. He was looking beyond Lebanon to other countries where civil wars meant unvaccinated child populations.

Because the fighting in Lebanon reached everywhere and never let up, there had been no countrywide immunization for at least five years. The central health ministry office was a shell. Except in a few private hospitals, the case reporting system was moribund. Nobody knew how many children were dying from the vaccine preventable diseases. What was feared most by health professionals working with the UNICEF office was a measles epidemic in the winter. This spurred Jim's thinking. Measles runs in cycles, and in towns and cities with high population density it can kill and handicap unvaccinated young children faster than any other communicable childhood infection. The general malnutrition in the country would make the impact even worse.

I was in charge of the UNICEF regional office in Amman at the time. For once I wasn't too far behind Jim. The thought of an immunization campaign in Lebanon came to both of our minds at about the same time. We imagined three rounds of four days each in the fall, separated by a month each. We pictured not just the blessing and support of the factions and militias, but their active participation. Flowers sticking out of gun barrels! An 80 per cent immunization target for the country – 80 per cent of the country's under-fives vaccinated with all the shots and their repeats. Better coverage than the USA.

We discussed it in his office in New York in May, 1987. 1 could tell that the bug had bitten him.

'What do you think, Richard ? Can they stop? These militias. I mean, do they have the communication and chain of command?'

'Oh yes. They can stop on a dime. They've bought all the electronics there are.'

'That was the problem in China. Bad communications or none. Especially the Nationalists, and there we were between the lines, trying to get food to starving people... Do you think they would stop?'

'I don't know. I hope so.'

'I think they might, Richard. They're religious people. The Shiites. Sheikh Fadlallah. The Maronites. Also, I think they're probably tired of being the world's...'

'Thugs. Crazy gunners.'

'Thugs. After all, it's been more than ten years, hasn't it? I expect most of them are family men. They read the European newspapers, they watch European TV... What will you tell them?'

*'I won't. Raymond or André will. They could go to Berri or Gemayel and say,
'Why can't Lebanon stand tall for a while, and prove it's not the sewer of the
world?' '*

'Too strong, Richard.' He grinned. *'The schools?'*

*'Can open up easily to be vaccination points. It will be a thrill for the
teachers.'*

'Going back to school?'

'Getting back to school after all these years!'

'And the media?'

*'The media are the most sophisticated in the region. They're dying to do
something constructive. The vaccines can come by boat from Cyprus, or better,
by road from Damascus, because we absolutely need to make Syria an owner
of this. The country's so small you don't need much of a cold chain.'*

'Pretty good, Richard.'

'We have a good teacher.'

'Okay, onward and upward! We'll stay in touch.'

Jim Grant radiated such inspirational karma and created such trust that
there were hundreds of UNICEF staff who would climb any mountain at his
bidding. In this he absolutely stood out among the other UN heads of agency
– only the late Brad Morse of UNDP had the gift.

Jim reached out and connected with everyone he met – the shy and the
surly, the high and the low. He put nervous new heads of state at ease; you
could see them relax and begin to smile. He was wonderful with frightened
children. But it seemed that he saved the best for staff at all levels – especially
field staff. He learned and remembered their names and those of their wives
and children. He looked out for them. Tears came to his eyes when he learned
they were ill or hurt. Staff sacrifices always impressed him. The toil and risk in
the lives of national staff – local UNICEF programme officers, drivers, others
impressed him particularly.

'You know,' I remember him saying, *'these people are amazing, aren't they?
They're our backbone! The internationals come and go every few years, they
get evacuated, but it's these people, the nationals, who stay on and keep
slogging. God knows where UNICEF would be without them.'*

One of them was Raymond Naimy.

Naimy, a Lebanese engineer, was UNICEF's resident programme officer in
Beirut. He was the effective head of the office when the idea of a national
immunization campaign in Lebanon began to take shape. There probably

wouldn't have been a campaign idea if Raymond hadn't been there. He and Jim went back years. The improbable work of Raymond's emergency repair teams in Beirut from the early '80s onward was one of UNICEF's brightest achievements before the Child Survival and Development Revolution caught on. Raymond and his teams worked under artillery and sniper fire to mend broken water mains and put damaged pumping stations back in operation. The work never ended; pipes and equipment would be smashed, cobbled back into working order, and smashed again. For one stretch of about two years, the UNICEF teams were Beirut's water supply department. If the water ran, it was because of them.

Raymond Naimy got to be known by the militia commanders and their leaders. When it suited them, they agreed to stop shooting for several hours so that he and his teams could finish the repairs. It was seen by all that, like few people with leverage in Beirut, Raymond had no agenda except to keep the water running. In the city's unreal circumstances, a kind of badge of honour attached to this work, and it attached to UNICEF.

It was on this reputation that Jim Grant pinned his hopes for a national immunization campaign – a plan that needed to win over all the factions. All of them and their client populations had suffered dry days and then drunk Raymond's water and been glad of it. Raymond, with these contacts, would be the campaign's natural point man and organizing focus. Of course he did not know this yet.

This writer and a UNICEF colleague, Andre Roberfroid, flew from Amman on a June day in 1987 to take the campaign scheme to Raymond. It was a trip usually made by road through Syria and the Chouf Mountains to keep a low profile. As we got off the plane in Beirut we learned that yet another hostage kidnapping – the snatching of a western journalist – had taken place two hours earlier on the road from the airport.

Raymond met us, polite, smiling, relaxed. The embodiment of Mr. Cool.

'How's Mr. Grant?'

'Tearing around like always. Sends his best.'

He took us to his banged-up sedan outside the terminal, explaining that hijackers weren't interested in ugly cars. We drove into the city. And then Raymond took us around and around in circles for an hour. At one point we came up against a tank in an alley.

'I took Mr. Grant a safer way,' he laughed.

'What's so special about Mr. Grant?'

'Oh, you know. He's kind of like a god to the staff. To my wife... Was it three rounds of immunization he's asking for? I think we can do it. We'll do it.'

'The staff have never done any mass immunization here, have they?'

'That's right.' The three of us pondered this.

'Doesn't matter. It's your water credentials with the faction leaders that Mr. Grant's counting on.'

'Oh, my,' he laughed. *'That man.'*

Raymond Naimy's access to the decision-makers was even better than Jim had hoped. Within days, he and André began to meet with Beirut's shakers and movers – the Christian Falange leader, Gemayel, Nabih Berri of the Shiites, the Druze leader Walid Jumblatt in his redoubt, Sheikh Fadlallah of the Party of God, the heads of the Orthodox and Roman Catholic Churches.

As they made their rounds to the fortified villas, past the snipers and bodyguards, the two UNICEF men encountered surprise and a kind of relief. In one way or another, all the leaders conceded that immunization across the country was a good idea, a righteous idea, especially if it might stave off an epidemic. Raymond and André told them, as Jim Grant had suggested, that more unvaccinated children could die in the winter from measles and other vaccine preventable diseases than had died in the whole war up to then. There was skepticism from the military commanders, who feared that the other factions would take tactical advantage of the breaks in the fighting. Raymond was able to convince them that this wouldn't happen because of the inter-locking nature of the ceasefire.

In August 1987, all the Beirut staff – water engineers, social workers, refugee camp officers, drivers – spent two to three weeks in training, learning the ins and outs of an immunization campaign. They did field trials in quiet neigh-borhoods to practice what they had learned. Government and private doctors, nurses, NGO members, and teachers were brought into the training. An upbeat, hugely effective television and radio buildup bracketed the country from late August. Door-to-door household surveys located and enumerated all under fives. The country was divided into manageable zones, each zone was put in charge of an immunization team with a roster of infants and children to be vaccinated, and vaccination stations were designated and readied. These stations were schools, mosques, and churches as often as they were health centres. The militias and private armies understood that they would have a main backup role in transport and communications. In Damascus, the commander of the Syrian army in Lebanon pledged his support.

On the eve of the first round of the campaign, all the gears seemed ready to mesh. In New York, Jim Grant met to review the Lebanon initiative with UN Secretary General, Perez de Cuellar, and two of his under secretaries. He took from the Secretary General a letter to the Lebanese Prime Minister, saluting the immunization campaign as a signal of human priority and hope to the world. The letter was put in this writer's hand for delivery. I took it to Prime Minister Salim el Hoss on 21 September, 1987 – the first day of the first campaign round.

'Maybe this will be a step in a direction no one can imagine yet,' he said, reading the text. *'We need to hope so.'* He looked up.

'I expect this was Mr. Grant's idea.'

It all held together. The days of tranquility kept Lebanon at peace for four days in September and four more each in October and November. The armed roadblocks at the Green Line and in the fortified neighborhoods gave way and opened up. Cold boxes and vaccine carriers were hauled across boundaries that had only been crossed by tanks and tracer bullets before. Gunmen did put flowers in the barrels of their AK-47s – this writer saw them. Naturally there were hitches. For all of Raymond Naimy's teams' alphabetized scheduling and prior notice to parents, mothers and fathers still mobbed some vaccination stations and created chaos during the first days of the first round. But after that, and in October and November, the campaign ran like a clock. Eighty two per cent of the under fives were fully immunized. There was no measles outbreak in Lebanon that winter.

'Well, what do you think, Boss?'

Jim Grant looked at us.

'I think we have to take our hats off to Raymond and his team. One more down – how many to go? Onward and upward! Come on over here to the map. Let's look at this region of yours.'

Iraq

We watched as they waved Yevgeny Primakov through the Iranian border crossing at Karan with as little fanfare as possible. He was coming out of Iraq after the last failed Russian persuasion mission to Saddam Hussein. His two cars with the darkened windows left on the road back to Tehran just as we were checking through with our UN passports, headed the other way.

We were a mixed UNICEF-WHO team of seven – four doctors, a nutritionist, a water engineer, and the UNICEF regional director. Waiting with us that morning, 16 February, 1991, were 15 Iranian drivers, 12 long haul trailer trucks loaded with 52 tons of emergency supplies for children and mothers, and the three land cruisers that had led our convoy out of Tehran and across the Zagros Mountains the day before. We had stopped for the night at the provincial town of Bakhtaran, short of the border, in order to be at the crossing the following day at a good hour. In the little hotel there, I spoke by satellite phone with Jim Grant in New York and learned that the allied command in Riyadh had agreed to stop bombing for a six hour period the next day. This was long enough for us to take the convoy from the border and across the desert to Baghdad.

'Well, good luck, Richard,' Jim said. 'You can go in peace. This is a wonderful opportunity. Godspeed!'

Jim Grant's decision to send a child relief mission into Baghdad at the height of the Gulf War seemed rash to many. Saddam Hussein might spurn the gesture. Or welcome it with open arms to try to use it to his own propaganda advantage. There was the element of physical risk. Bombs were failing. Would mission members become collateral damage statistics? CNN and Peter Arnett were giving the world non stop coverage of what was happening under the bombing – the country blacked out, people foraging for food, a civilian bomb shelter incinerated. From this, though, a sense that 'the other side' might need and deserve emergency help was also beginning to dawn in Europe and America.

Jim shared with me in January 1991, his own sense of how fast the quality of life in Baghdad must be falling. Iraq had been an energy-dependent country with high-tech habits. He knew that an average of 1,100 Iraqi babies were being born everyday, and that Iraqi's medical stocks were low because of the Health Ministry's dependence on constant re-supply by air from Europe. From messages brought to Amman by Iraqi UNICEF staff, he learned that the country was down to its last days of child vaccines and childbirth supplies. There was no running water, either. All six water purification and pumping plants were down for the duration. Toilets had stopped working. Much of the population was drawing water for cooking and home use from the Tigris River, which was also being used as a waste sluice. No one in the allied leadership had had a civilian disaster in mind when the air war started, but one was happening. How serious was it? What could be done to reach the vulnerable, especially the children, and put some kind of life back into the health system?

Jim kept his finger on the political pulse at the same time. He was in touch by phone with editorial offices, NGOs, donor embassies, the State Department, and UNICEF national committees around the world to get a feeling for public opinion. Through close contacts like President Mubarak of Egypt he sounded out the Arab reaction.

As his thinking began to crystallize, Jim indirectly reached another old acquaintance, one of the most sensitively placed – Tariq Aziz. Two years earlier, as the Iraq-Iran war was ending, I had stood by in Baghdad as Jim joked and reviewed common experiences with the Foreign Minister. Jim was in Aziz's office then to finalize the hand over of 300 Japanese jeeps he had personally obtained from Tokyo to rebuild and extend Iraq's child health infra-structure, particularly vaccination stations and primary health care training centres. That big gift out of the blue had made an impression on the Iraqi leadership. The Aziz connection minimized the prospect of mischief from Baghdad.

There were still miles to go. The Secretary General, Perez de Cuellar, was convinced of the rightness of the mission, but beneath him were layers of nay-saying and uncertainty. LIN partner agencies, including some whose mandates corresponded most closely to Iraq's critical needs, had to be dragged into agreement. Valuable time passed as Jim and this writer traveled about, making the case that Iraqi children were not to be confused with the Republican Guard. A few members of the LIN Sanctions Committee in New York bitterly fought the mission, insisting to Jim that our delivery of high-energy biscuits, vaccines, and midwife kits could provide Saddam Hussein with war material. But one by one the obstacles evaporated, and Jim had a green light.

It was nearing noon when the last of the drivers checked their loads, and the eight foot wide white LIN markings on the roofs of their trailer rigs, and rolled off onto the highway to Baghdad. The departure was two hours behind schedule but the sky was overcast and we were nervously confident that Jim Grant's bargain with Riyadh would hold. We knew we were being observed. Over our own road noise we could often hear the rumble of fighter jets criss-crossing overhead.

The only sign of war we could see for four hours as we passed villages, towns, and empty desert was the blackened wreckage of electrical power stations. Every one seemed to have been bombed to the ground. There was no vehicle traffic on the four-lane highway, but in all directions we could see people carrying buckets and jerry cans for water.

Jim Grant had worked out with the Iraqis a tight protocol for the security and distribution of the supplies we brought. Sticking to this, we left the highway at Baquba, outside Baghdad, and parked the trucks for offloading at a main medical storage depot presumably near no bomb targets. Two of our group stayed there to monitor the process. The rest of the team proceeded to Baghdad in the land cruisers.

At five in the evening we were at the El Rashid Hotel, which was to be the team's base for the week of this mission. We located the CNN work space in the hotel basement and used their satellite hookup to call Jim Grant.

'Everyone OK? No air action on the road? Wonderful! You're watching the offloading? Great! We did it, didn't we? Be careful. Make the most of it.'

An hour or two later, the sky lit up and the bombing resumed and continued for three hours.

At first light the next morning and for each of the six days that followed, the UN team fanned out across Baghdad, the suburbs, and into the south, visiting homes, health stations, markets, water installations, and hospitals, asking questions and filling our notebooks. In the evenings at the El Rashid we compared and combined notes by candlelight. Afterward, on the basement satellite phone, we sent summaries back to Jim Grant and, as we heard his pencil scratch, I could picture him filling another of the small brown pocket-sized notepads he used to buy by the dozen at the grocery store.

We saw strange sights and appalling ones. Small boys flying kites and nonchalantly skipping about during daylight air raids; older children refusing to leave the sides of their parents, clutching at their sleeves; in the midst of an otherwise untouched downtown area that reminded me of Los Angeles, high mounds of dark rubble that had once been the national telecommunications complex; well-dressed people carrying home tree branches they had pulled off in the park; the smoking cavity of the hotel-size Amiria bomb shelter, its rubble still hot enough underfoot to be felt through one's shoes.

Skeptics had warned Jim Grant before the mission that a supply delivery to Baghdad would be a dangerous, high profile gesture making no difference in the end. They were wrong. After the convoy had unloaded, Health Ministry inventories showed 60 to 80 per cent increases in stocks of vaccines, syringes, midwife kits, and selected essential drugs. Team members surveyed and confirmed this. The new vaccines and syringes were put to work immediately in an emergency epidemic control programme. Included also in the convoy's delivery were scores of emergency medical kits, each containing the crisis supplies, drugs and surgical tools a doctor would need to serve 10,000 people for three months.

Beyond the emergency supplies, the mission had a catalytic effect in opening up Iraq and laying out the country's humanitarian needs. What the team members first diagnosed, and conveyed in their mission report, provided a basic map of conditions and needs that would be used by university study teams and other assistance groups that arrived in Iraq over the following weeks and months. The mission's findings also had an effect in causing the Sanctions Committee in New York to ease some of its main restrictions. Much of what Jim Grant had hoped the mission might achieve was already working like yeast.

Jim always preached that the only way to reach UNICEF's objectives for children was to build up political will. That was everything. He saw the Iraq mission as a way to build global political will. This happened. More reports came back, a tide of public concern began to rise, Croatia and Bosnia came into the news, and politicians paid attention.

Later that year, the halls of the UN General Assembly buzzed with talk about the world's obligation to put the lives of the innocent before state sovereignty. Speeches were made. A European foreign minister said that the right to intervene in war for humanitarian ends was *'the most truly innovative concept of the remaining decade of this century.'* It was Jim Grant's concept they were talking about.

The President's necktie

The din was huge and the wide reception room seemed small as a crowd of the great and good milled around the White House Christmas tree. In the midst of it, taking congratulations, talking over the noise, his face alight, was Jim Grant.

It was 21 December, 1993. The event was the launching of *The State of World's Children Report,* with President Clinton standing by to give it his special blessing. Jim was showing people his Save the Children necktie, a lively confection that always provoked comment. It gave him a handy advocacy pretext with people he was meeting for the first time.

Presently an Oval Office aide appeared at Jim's shoulder and invited him to come to a nearby alcove for a brief chat with the President before the ceremony. Jim excused himself and followed. As Jim and the aide re-told it, this is what happened in the alcove.

'Mr. Grant, welcome! And congratulations. I'd hoped we could talk a little before we go out there. I'm one of your biggest fans.'

'Thank you very much, Mr. President. You're making this a big day for us.'

'Say, I like that tie of yours! Where did you get it?'

'Save the Children. If you like it, you can have it.' (Begins to remove tie.) 'Here, put it on. You can wear it to the ceremony. It'll be a big hit.'

'Well, sure. You're right.' (Laughs.) 'Here.' (Removes his tie.) 'You can take mine. Not bad, huh?'

That was how Jim Grant left the White House wearing the President's tie. We never saw it on him again. Millions and millions watching TV must have seen Jim's on the President that day, though. Staff weren't sure who came out of the exchange best. Jim apparently found a re-supply channel, because a few days later he was back sporting the tie with the daisy chain of children splashed across it.

Controversy and continuity: programming for women in Jim Grant's UNICEF

by Mary Racelis

Jim Grant's leadership of UNICEF provoked many a controversy over UNICEF programme priorities but none more consistently contentious than that of women. This essay traces the evolution of Grant's thinking on women as a strategic group in promoting UNICEF's mandate for children, and details the policy-action outcomes under his leadership. It also tries to convey what it was like to have Jim as a boss and a friend.

When Jim Grant took over as Executive Director in 1980, UNICEF's orientation to women in developing countries centred on their mother role. After all, reasoned executive board and staff alike, UNICEF was a children's organization. Improving women's health and nutritional status was important largely because their children would be better off from conception through infancy and childhood. As Maggie Black expressed it in her history of the organization, *'UNICEF accepted as a matter of course that the well-being of infants and children was inseparable from the well-being of those in whose wombs they were conceived.'*

By the time Grant left the organization 15 years later, he had engineered a conceptual and programmatic transformation in UNICEF, moving it from the narrow perspective of women primarily as mothers, to one which embraced women's mainstream economic and other roles, their status and rights, and, in his last three years, the girl child. Not only did women require assistance with pregnancy, lactation and childcare; they also merited support as income earners, community service providers, local and national leaders, and potentially active citizens in governance. With the focus on the girl child, UNICEF's concerns for children appeared at last to have achieved an integration with the broader concerns for gender equity over the whole life cycle and indeed for future generations.

But to the last, Jim considered this wider perspective valid only because it made women better child nurturers and protectors. He never did accept the worldwide feminist position emphasizing equity, rights and choice, and which asserted that conceptually and programmatically UNICEF should start by addressing women as women and then support the motherhood, or child-related, aspects of their lives. That, he felt, went beyond UNICEF's mandate. While attention to the girl child was hailed by women's rights and mother-child advocates alike, the former were apprehensive that this convergence might distract UNICEF's attention from its women-supportive programmes.

The issue of how to deal with women and gender concerns in UNICEF programmes was never fully resolved from the perspectives of most women and some male allies within the organization and on the Executive Board. Jim's stance drew continuing criticism from sister organization, the UN Population Fund (UNFPA) throughout the incumbency of Executive Director Nafis Sadik, a strong advocate for women's rights including their roles as mothers.

Women as women versus the mother–child focus

Part of Jim's resistance to the feminist or women's rights and choices perspective stemmed from his associating it with western middle class women, whom he saw as rejecting or de-emphasizing motherhood roles, even as most developing country women continued to defend them. Perhaps his being a member of a generation whose middle and upper class men valued women primarily as helpmates and mothers, and only secondarily in roles outside the home, accounts for some of his difficulties. His first wife, Ethel, was a social worker in Washington, caring for children with learning difficulties. Ethel also spent much of her adult life being a caring partner to Jim, resigning from her job three years after Jim was appointed to UNICEF to join him full time in his work for children, until her sudden passing on their trip to India in 1988. Ethel played a strong supportive role, establishing warm relations with staff and their families and often serving as a channel for ideas and complaints which staff members were hesitant to raise directly with Jim. Through Ethel, invitations to breakfast conferences in the 'Roof House' soon became coveted entries to gracious and productive gatherings at their home as the work day began.

Since UNICEF programmes operated in developing countries, Jim felt he was reinforcing the less strident or more muted voices there of women actively engaged in promoting women's child nurturing roles. While he deserves recognition for that principled stance, it must be said that he never came to terms with the evolving feminist discourse articulated by activist NGO grassroots female and male workers rather than by local elites. Theirs was an orientation that, like feminism worldwide, highlighted choice and empowerment for developing country women, but focused on the poor and powerless women and children among them. These pro-women activist groups saw no contradiction in pursuing a women's empowerment approach that would strengthen a woman's decision to give priority to her children's needs if that was her choice. The key was to focus on a woman's own priorities (which in any case usually gave high priority to children's well-being), rather than decide for her that her children must come first. A woman had a right to be the person she wanted to be, and not be forced into carrying out male-defined stereotypes of who she was or ought to be.

The controversy persisted throughout Jim's incumbency, with most of the women professional staff, along with some male colleagues, staunchly advocating women's empowerment and choices as the *sine qua non* of programming for children, and Grant apprehensive that this approach did not relate in some defined way to children. In his last years as Executive Director, the debate became somewhat muted when the girl child took centre stage. Feminists approved of its intellectual underpinnings and female focus. UNICEF was acknowledging that gender discrimination could be eradicated only if action was sustained over the entire lifecycle, beginning with the girl fetus in the womb, the baby, the toddler, the young child, the older child, the adolescent – right through adulthood and old age.

While these iterations of female life stages had always been implicit in pre-Grant policy reviews, transforming 'young girls' into 'the girl child' represented a significant intellectual and programmatic shift. The new orientation emphasized that girls had a right to compete successfully with boys for society's attention and to gain access to their fair share of resources, skills, and knowledge. Accordingly, feminists were willing to suspend for the time being their insistence on women's empowerment and choices as the central programme focus in favour of promoting an equitable start in life for girls. Jim Grant could not have been happier.

As for my own relationship with Jim, it was one of mutual respect and admiration. Since he was trained as an economist and I as a sociologist, our frameworks for thinking about society sometimes clashed. Although we had some contact from the start through my women's development role, it was only at the first high level UNICEF consultation in Sterling Forest that I came seriously to his attention. Why, I queried before the participants, was UNICEF paying so much attention to abstract models being promulgated by economists, while giving only lukewarm support to community participation? Development after all is about people and their actions. Ever after that, when he mentioned the word 'participation' he would look at me with a twinkle in his eye, and smile remembering my David-like challenge to the World Bank's Goliath at Sterling Forest.

The next time he noticed me quite specifically was when I became Chairperson of the Global Staff Association. My firm but reasonable stance in staff matters earned his approval, and my insistence on staff participation in high level committees appealed to his democratic persuasions. Once I became a regional director, he expected me, along with the others, to be his voice in the field but also to be a voice for the field people in New York. He counted on us to defend him in outside circles but to 'tell it like it is' inside, complete with solutions.

Our friendship flourished along with our professional relationship for 15 years. We liked and respected each other. When he gave a speech in my honour at the 65th birthday party in New York organized for me by my children, I realized yet again how lucky I was to have been a part of Jim Grant's UNICEF. He was a man of vision and principle, an intellectual but also pragmatic leader who inspired masses of people, UNICEF staff among them, to work tirelessly for children's and women's well-being. He was truly a friend, whose memory I cherish.

Working with Jim Grant in New York

Executive Director Harry Labouisse's last year with UNICEF coincided with my first year as Senior Adviser for Family and Child Welfare in New York. My predecessor, Titi Memet, had been recruited in the mid-seventies to develop the family planning aspects of maternal and child health. In the logic of that era, emerging women's concerns were routed to her for attention. Given the exponentially expanding activities around women generated by the 1975

International Woman's Year in Mexico, Titi as Senior Adviser for Family Welfare, found herself thrust ever more deeply into the *de facto* women's adviser role. She convinced the Board to create several new regional advisers posts based in the regional offices.

When UNICEF invited me to take over the job upon her assumption of the representative's post in Pakistan, it was an offer I could not resist. Think of all the exciting possibilities for moving women's issues forward worldwide! Immediately upon joining UNICEF, I attached 'Children's Welfare' to my Senior Policy Specialist title to enable me to break free of the implicit family planning thrust. Later I added 'Women's Development' and still later 'Community Participation' to my title as expressions of what I really wanted to promote in UNICEF.

In a sense, field offices were more progressive than headquarters in already having designated women's advisers in four regions. Other regions allocated a country programme officer the same region-wide mandate. Their tasks were to articulate women's issues and help country offices formulate and carry out programmes for women. Parallel and newly constituted knowledge networks helped formalize common interest across regions and justified bringing these regional focal points as well as strong women programme officers from country offices to New York to sharpen UNICEF's policy, programming and advocacy for women. It was this core of articulate pro-women advocates in an informal worldwide network that was ready and waiting for Jim Grant upon his arrival in New York.

The new Executive Director

Jim hit the ground running. Having served as Chair of the United States delegation to the UNICEF Board meeting in Mexico City in 1979, he had already demonstrated to the staff in attendance his keen understanding of developing country needs and issues. Here was a man of ideas and action. Clearly, he was determined to take UNICEF to new heights and make the world pay attention to children.

Staff and country delegations who had become accustomed to the genteel, diplomatic and fatherly style of Harry Labouisse did not quite know what to make of this energetic, persuasive, and informal (*'Call me Jim!'*) Executive Director. Jim believed that action-oriented UNICEF could and should become the UN's most effective agency, even if to get there it sometimes had to ride roughshod over the traditional niceties of international civil service and diplomatic convention. Indeed, some cynics projected the image of the 'bull in the china shop' plunging through the aisles upsetting masses of delicate glassware and leaving shards behind without so much as a backward glance as he raced forward.

Rumour had it that the new Executive Director favoured previously unheard of breakfast conferences with staff and delegates, complete with bagels and cream cheese applied with plastic knives and coffee in plastic thermal cups. To those reared in the delicate art of traditional diplomacy, this incorporation of everyman democracy into their international lifestyles proved almost too much. And to compound the problem, the new Executive Director didn't even speak French!

The 1980 Executive Board and the UN Women's Conference, Copenhagen

The need for Jim Grant to articulate UNICEF's perspectives on women came early, owing to the impending United Nations Mid-Decade Conference for Women scheduled for Copenhagen in mid-1980. UNICEF's task, like that of countries and all UN agencies, was to assess progress in its programme and advocacy activities, and lay out its future strategies. A parallel requirement mandated the preparation of a UNICEF policy paper on women and development for the Executive Board, with essentially the same data being compiled for both Copenhagen and New York. The approval of the women's paper by the Board would strengthen its subsequent presentation at the UN Conference.

Information was pouring in following a questionnaire I had sent out to country and regional offices. My small staff and I synthesized and analyzed the reports, trying to integrate the data with existing UNICEF policies and new thinking on women's development. We welcomed Grant's offer to have sociologist Hoda Badran, the Middle East and North Africa Regional Adviser on Women, work with us toward the end of our report preparations, since none of us had had direct experience as UNICEF programme officers in the field. We knew the paper would benefit from her being temporarily detailed to us.

Reading our first draft Hoda felt that, as a newcomer, I had been intimidated by male colleagues in the Programme Division, who still clung to traditional stereotypes of women. (At the time I was one of the very few women professionals in the organization.) It was time, said Hoda, to be more critical of UNICEF's programmes, which extolled the mother role and women's housewifely interests through support to sewing, knitting, crocheting, and cooking classes. These non-income-generating housewifely skills merely reinforced women's limited options and narrow images of their potential, serving only to enrich the manufacturers of sewing machines, knitting and crochet needles, and cooking stoves.

Although women's advancement had long been on UNICEF's agenda, starting in the 1950s with support for women's training and taking a leap forward in 1964 when the transition to a development organization began, implementation had taken a decidedly middle class orientation. Programmes promoted motherly activities related to child-bearing needs, featuring health and nutrition education, and volunteer community work through mothers' clubs and daycare centres. Inspired by Hoda's criticism of field programmes and her commitment to developing country interpretations of women's rights and roles, we helped her rewrite the paper.

Thus, her version was the one circulated to the regional advisers and the informal women's network that convened in New York to review the new paper. Most agreed with its progressive orientation. It was time for UNICEF to recognize the vibrant discourse being generated by women worldwide and join the global bandwagon for genuine women's equality and development. The connection with children had to be couched in this framework.

With such strong backing I felt sufficiently protected. Field participants returned to their posts, pleased at having generated a document that would at last enable UNICEF to make a quantum leap forward for women and the children they nurtured. They in turn could hold their heads up high in women's circles. Next steps entailed circulating the draft document mainly to senior officers in the Programme Division for review and comment – some revision if necessary – before it was sent on for final editing to the Office of the Secretary of the Board. At the same time, we responded to the requests of women members on key Board delegations to read advance copies of the draft. These were women with whom I had earlier discussed the report.

I still remember vividly how stunned I was when the Programme Division's all-male reviewers returned the document to me soon after, asking for substantial revisions. The outlook, they pointed out, was too radical and the language unnecessarily strong. Both had to be toned down. Resentment and anger erupted in the women's network when they received this message.

I tried, only minimally successfully, to negotiate some compromises with my New York male colleagues, but their authority prevailed. The final version was distributed in a considerably watered down form.

Jim participated only peripherally in this debate. His own plate was full as he prepared for his first Board meeting, with a new and creative budget proposal to be approved. This featured several new high level posts aimed at bringing strong intellectual backing to UNICEF's action orientation. Additional controversy over a sensitive topic like women was, therefore, hardly needed. Presumably, then, he simply went along with the advice of his senior lieutenants at headquarters and authorized the watered down text of the women's paper.

Soon after the Executive Board opened, women delegates who had seen the earlier version attacked the paper before them as bland and woefully deficient. It failed to address the exciting new intellectual and developmental climate on women. Specifically mentioned was the more progressive draft document which had been informally shared with them earlier on. They demanded to know the reasons why it had been changed so drastically – and for the worse!

This event was not entirely spontaneous. The story can now be told. The women Board members and some UNICEF women's network members had met immediately before the Board opening for an update on trends and perspectives within the organization regarding women. There the Board delegates had learned that the progressive stance of the earlier paper had been rejected. They assured us that they would raise the issues at the Board.

Quoting favorably portions of the earlier text during the Board debate, and insisting that the progressive text rather than the paper in front of them represent UNICEF's policy and programme outlooks, the women delegates won the day. The Board affirmed that notable points in the earlier women's network text would constitute UNICEF's submission to the Copenhagen conference. Thus, as they have done for centuries, women outside the seats of power maneuvered around their male authority figures, linking up in sister-hood with women in power to dramatize a common grievance. It was a heady and exhilarating victory for us all.

As a result, UNICEF policy made a quantum conceptual and programme leap forward. It still acknowledged the importance of mother roles but also affirmed a more holistic perspective incorporating multi-dimensional roles. In programme terms, this justified income generation and credit schemes for women, and training them in leadership and new and non-traditional skills. UNICEF staff, male and female, would be held accountable for implementing this new thrust. The women's network was ecstatic. They now had a basis for persuading, even insisting if not demanding, that recalcitrant male colleagues develop programmes corresponding to the new Board directives on women. The task ahead of me would require writing programme directives in support of this.

In Copenhagen, UNICEF received high praise for its enlightened stance – an orientation which, several delegates pointed out, was not widely evident in the other also male-dominated UN agencies. As the new Executive Director, Jim reaped the benefit of these Mid-Decade Conference accolades. At the same time, the Board debate had alerted him to the strategic importance of women as mobilizers on the world stage. Ever a political animal, he went to Copenhagen prepared. In his speech to the assembly, he emphasized that,'A woman's right to share whatever fruits the process of economic development has to offer is absolutely fundamental to all her roles.' Pointing out that the process of modernization had relegated women to the margins of economic life, often leaving them poorer and worse off than before, he stated, 'We now accept that the issue of women's rights is central to the whole process of development.' His Board-derived assertions painted a broad picture of the actions that would have to be taken by leaders and planners in developing countries so that women are welcomed as partners and agents in the decision making process.

At the same time he resisted the prospect of placing UNICEF at the forefront of the effort of women's enhancement in the UN system. Fearing that would derail UNICEF's mandate for children, he opted for the partner role within the UN family and among NGOs. The dichotomy of women versus mothers still loomed large in his mind. While ever afterwards he showed a deep commitment to promoting women's roles and rights, it was also clear that his first commitment was always to improving the lives of children, and from that came a solid commitment to improving the lives of women. But when all was said and done, UNICEF was about children.

The female circumcision issue

Only the female circumcision issue dampened Jim's success – and mine – at Copenhagen. My first task at UNICEF in 1979 had been to write its programme directives on the subject, drawing on completed survey forms sent in by field staff. Since I had never even heard of female circumcision before I got to New York, my learning curve rose quickly, boosted by reams of field reports.

Ironically, both Jim and I went to the Conference confident that UNICEF was in the forefront of international efforts to call attention to the problem. We were the first UN agency to issue programme guidelines to UNICEF staff on female circumcision (now referred to as 'genital mutilation'), informing them of its drastic effects on girls and women. Recommendations addressing mainly the health consequences stressed that it was the practicing societies that had to take the lead in confronting the problem, given socio-cultural sensitivities. For the operation was associated by men and women alike with the positive value of preserving women's chastity, and with the symbolism of girls' coming of age.

The Nordic delegations in particular, who saw this as a global equity issue, lauded UNICEF for its courageous and forthright initiative. Even though some believed we had not sufficiently condemned the practice, they nonetheless praised UNICEF's stance. The subject came to a head at an NGO Forum round-table we had organized on female circumcision. The praise turns out to have been short-lived.

A number of African women participants roundly criticized UNICEF, not because they supported female circumcision, but because they deplored our placing the subject in the international limelight for condemnation by the entire world. The appropriate strategy, they told us, would have been to enable Africans, especially women, to deal with the problem without undue interference from northern groups. Grant felt embarrassed and vulnerable, while I was distressed at not having anticipated the situation. He never chided me for that, however.

It was with a great deal of satisfaction some few years later that, as a regional director in Africa, I had the privilege of supporting a dynamic, continent-wide African NGO organized around the elimination of harmful traditional practices, female circumcision being a major one. Gradually the members were moving from the portrayal of female circumcision as largely a health issue to incorporating gender concerns into the debate.

As for Jim, he subsequently avoided this issue partly because of its association with feminist platforms and the discomfort most males felt discussing it. In his view, such female-specific matters were best left to programme officers and technical policy specialists like myself. He was moving fast on the child survival and development highway and did not want to get embroiled in distracting controversies. However, he enjoined us to brief him immediately if any serious problems on the subject loomed that might catch him off guard. He did not like surprises.

Women as advocates for child survival and development

The Mid-Decade Conference had a profound impact on Jim Grant. It helped him recognize the power of women when they organize around an issue. They were the force he needed to power his new Child Survival and Development Revolution. In pursuit of this aim, he recruited Lucille Mair to become UNICEF's Special Adviser on Women upon the completion of her assignment as the Secretary General of the UN Mid-Decade Conference.

To many, including myself, the appointment initially appeared to duplicate my position as the women's adviser. Jim asked me to see him in order to explain his decision. He knew I would wonder whether he was unhappy with my work. His explanation emphasized that the move had nothing to do with my competence or performance. Lucille had the credibility of a high ranking UN official, who was also from a developing country, and had a high profile worldwide from her leadership of the Copenhagen conference. Her expertise and status were exactly what he needed to galvanize women for the Child Survival and Development Revolution.

In the light of Lucille's entry, I asked Grant whether I could change my function and title to Senior Policy Specialist, Community Participation and Family Welfare. That way I could still work with country office programmes on women and their participation in community life. Lucille's high level advocacy for enhancing women's development and linking it to child survival and development would not be compromised. Jim remembered well from Sterling Forest that community participation represented my overriding professional and personal interest.

My finding a win-win solution to a potentially awkward situation came as a great relief to him. Being caught in conflicts among his senior staff was another of his great dislikes. I in turn greatly appreciated his concern for my feelings and his personal explanation as to why he was appointing Lucille Mair.

I then began setting up community based training workshops in Bangladesh, Peru and the Philippines. No sooner had one been successfully completed than Jim called me to his office. It was then that he told me of his intention to appoint me the Regional Director for East Africa.

The status of women as UNICEF staff

My having inherited Titi Memet's position at headquarters made me the logical person among New York's many talented and committed women to serve as focal point for staff issues around women. These encompassed recruitment to higher level positions, promotion, training opportunities, and sexual harassment. The worldwide drive for women's advancement and place-ment in decision making positions was on its way, and UNICEF was no exception. Perhaps because I became so much involved in staff matters and participated in important committees, as well as travelling widely to field offices in my technical role, I was elected Chairperson of the Global Staff Association in 1981.

Jim was pleased at this turn of events as he knew me to be a calm and flexible person. In his estimation, I would not cause him problems as GSA Chair. He also favoured my constantly bringing women's issues into almost any discussion underway. Strengthened by a remarkable set of officers, the GSA began systematically organizing around key staff concerns. Democratic participation in decision making with devolution of authority to committees led by the officers, half of them women, became known as the hallmarks of my management style. Jim approved. He understood the process as his own democratic instincts were strong.

The GSA in the early 1980s enjoyed a level of cooperation with the Executive Director that had never before happened to our knowledge. His door was open to us whenever we wanted to raise important issues with him. We soon learned, however, that if we did not propose solutions to the problems, his eyes would soon glaze over and his body language would signify that he was tuning out. Subsequent meetings found us better prepared. He responded by often agreeing to our requests, like asking the GSA Chairperson to speak at the Executive Board, appointing a GSA member, including more women, on key committees, inviting the Chairperson to be a member of the Executive Committee, taking more seriously promotion from within even as he brought in new faces at high levels in UNICEF, agreeing to study patterns of recruit-ment and promotion for women and taking affirmative action on their behalf.

By 1982, Jim had established a quota for women professionals. In 1994, the findings of an in-house study and excellent analysis undertaken by programme officer Eimi Watanabe convinced him of the need for actual targets. By 1990, he announced, 33 per cent of international professional positions would be filled by women. When the target was reached in 1990, he raised the figure to 40 per cent by 1995.

More women professionals were recruited, a number into higher level positions. Implementation details he left to the Division of Personnel to work out. Faced with the complexities of carrying out new instructions as well as occasional protests from aggrieved parties, the DOP Director considered the GSA Board member a thorn in his side. Sometimes we compromised when it seemed appropriate, but mostly we got our way. We liked to think that this was because our solid and well researched proposals were compelling and difficult to refute. More likely, it was Jim Grant's support to democratic staff relations that made the difference.

The breastfeeding controversy

The early 1980s saw the Child Survival and Development Revolution being hammered out at headquarters, and intensively discussed with regional directors, representatives, and other field-based staff. Jim was determined to change UNICEF from an organization with flexible, minimally-integrated and slowly evolving holistic programmes and projects for children to a dynamic, action oriented organization. Through the Child Survival and Development Revolution, he saw UNICEF as generating doable, measurable outcomes quickly. Not only would this bring quantifiable benefits to children; it would draw worldwide support, including donor interest, toward a rapidly accelerating worldwide movement. Reducing infant and child mortality through pragmatic, focused actions would be the key. Consultations with health, nutrition, and education experts on the 'doables' yielded GOBI-FFF: growth monitoring, oral rehydration therapy, immunization, breastfeeding, family planning, female education and food security.

A number of staff expressed skepticism at the strategy of singling out what looked like a return to narrow, vertical programmes for achieving the child survival and development objectives. After all, Alma Ata in 1978 had revitalized public health, which eschewed the curative and top down approaches of the past in favour of primary health care and a holistic orientation. UNICEF appeared to be betraying the primary health care orientation in championing only some of its parts selectively. Nonetheless, women advocates were relieved that female education and, to a lesser extent, family planning had been included. Growth monitoring, oral rehydration and food security were appropriate and gender neutral in terms of children's and family well-being,

The only controversial element among the seven was breastfeeding. Given the ongoing mother versus women struggle, the emphasis on breastfeeding appeared yet again to compartmentalize women around their maternal roles. Denunciations were rife: were women always to be portrayed in terms of their breasts and as the human equivalent of milking cows? Moreover, while breastfeeding was a desirable and natural practice, male advocates like Jim had to recognize that it was declining, not because women did not know any better, or not even primarily because the infant formula industry was strongly promoting bottle-feeding. It was declining because women had to work and could not breastfeed even if they wanted to. The prevailing situation in field, factory or market discouraged babies in the workplace, and certainly did not support women's going home to feed them. To the women's network, the breastfeeding campaign ignored the reality of women's lives, compounding that shortsightedness by castigating the victims – women – for turning to bottle-feeding.

The outcry peaked when UNICEF printed thousands of copies of a calendar featuring women of different nationalities breastfeeding a baby, one emotion generating picture per month. Had today's broader orientation in UNICEF been in place then instead of the mother focus, the breastfeeding calendar might not have created such a stir.

Where does one draw the line, asked Jim of his women staff, when it came to picturing women breastfeeding? It could be sensitively done, they replied, if only part of the breast was modestly shown and the baby and mother were given more space and attention than the breast itself. The baby sucking on the mother's nipple was acceptable, but exposed nipples were unacceptable! As a result of the outcry, most of the calendars were shipped to country offices, where breastfeeding women were commonplace scenes and free calendars of any kind were eagerly snapped up.

Much later, the Baby Friendly Hospital Initiative would draw similar fire. While the ten steps that would make a hospital 'baby friendly' were entirely appropriate, they failed to take into sufficient account the broader realities of poor women's lives. An attempt by women staff to promote ten steps for women to accompany those for the baby was never seriously considered. In developing countries, they argued, newly delivered women usually had to leave the maternity hospital the day after delivery to make room for the next new mother. She might be returning to a squalid hut in a city slum or have to go back to the backbreaking work of cultivating her farm plot, which is when she needed most help. How could really poor women be served by a baby friendly hospital, unless strategies for the crucial days after her departure were also covered?

After listening to this debate, Jim saw the point more clearly. Since our alternative formulation for baby and mother friendly centres expanded and improved on the original idea, he had no difficulty with the reorientation. It was another of those occasions where he recalled the story of the stubborn mule. When the mule would not budge despite pleas and entreaties from his owner, the exasperated owner gave his favorite animal a sharp blow with a 'two by four' piece of wood. The mule leaped forward and kept going. *'Sometimes,'* said Jim, *'you have to hit me with a two by four!'*

Evolving strategies for women

UNICEF's policies and programmes for women evolved with each new Senior Policy Specialist for Women. Jim generally went along with their perspectives, and listened carefully to my recommendations on candidates for the position. I was succeeded in New York in 1983 by Nadia Youssef who brought the orientation of mainstreaming women's concerns in society. She referred to women's economic activities, instead of the more common 'income generation,' as being more responsive to employment and increasingly complex and profitable business operations. In a poor but rapidly modernizing society, women's income generating projects all too often generated only small scale localized outputs with little connection to mainstream assets, processes, and services. In Africa, she would frequently point out, it was the women who were farmers. Once Jim understood what this meant, he took special delight, especially before African audiences, in referring to the African farmer as 'she'.

Women needed credit and technical assistance for savings and income. They would benefit from improved food production capacity through access to improved agricultural technology and skills. Small scale women's projects, long supported by UNICEF, needed to give way to activities that brought women real economic returns by integrating their efforts into the larger society, and indeed transforming that larger society to give value to women's contributions. A stronger economic role would also reduce women's dependency on others and lead to their liberation.

Further, women had to be seen in all the stages of their life cycle – as infants, girls, adolescents, young adults, older adults, and elderly women. This contrasted greatly with UNICEF's tendency to focus almost exclusively on women as young adults because that was when they were pregnant, lactating and raising young children. To improve women's lives, insisted Nadia Youssef, all stages of the journey had to be considered.

The Executive Board policy paper for 1985, which assessed the progress made since Copenhagen, detailed this strongly economic approach to women's enhancement. It also moved policy one step further by affirming support to women in their own right. The link between women and children remained but distinctions were made in terms of direct economic assistance and advocacy for women as women. It was the closest UNICEF came to accepting the dual mandate. The Board paper also served as the basic UNICEF document for the mid-1985 UN International Conference on Women in Nairobi, featuring an end-decade review.

The UN International Conference on Women in 1985

Scores of UNICEF women programme officers descended upon Nairobi for the UN International Conference, joining the thousands from all parts of the world and many African farmers and urban poor women from Kenya and the surrounding countries. The city exuded a heady atmosphere as women of all colours, shapes and sizes found common cause to celebrate sisterhood and look to the future. In Kenya, a diplomatic fiasco of sorts was avoided when Conference Secretary General, Letitia Shahani, saved the honour of women by taking her place on the dais as the lone women at the opening session of the Women's Conference.

In his speech to the delegates, Jim Grant described new possibilities for empowering women, and made one special request. He reaffirmed UNICEF's commitment, recently approved by its Executive Board, to strengthen and support actions that would yield direct social, health and economic benefits to women living in poverty for their own well-being. He also recognized the improvement of women's lives as being a necessary prerequisite to social development and child well-being. He went on to cite the potential for *'a revolution in child survival and health, largely through a new empowerment of women which could have major beneficial implications for women as well as for children.'*

UNICEF was moving forward on female education, reduction of women's workload, economic activities, food security and socio-economic activities at the household level promoting child survival and development. He strongly believed that empowering women with knowledge of child protection techniques would unleash not only a health revolution for children but greater confidence among women about their ability to control important aspects of their lives. When women realized that their actions could make a life or death difference for their children, this new awareness would transform their lives. He concluded with a special request, an appeal to women to spearhead the movement for child survival and development, mobilizing themselves and others to demand and to help achieve universal immunization of children and pregnant women by 1990.

To many of the northern feminists in the audience, this resonated as an all too familiar instrumental approach. Jim could never crack their resistance and court their cooperation on women as leaders for children's concerns. He was disturbed that women programme officers could not convince their northern counterparts, while we were equally upset that he could not seem to understand the problem. However, developing country women, especially African women, responded enthusiastically to his challenge. Their brand of feminism carried a higher level of comfort with children and motherhood than it did in northern women's rights. The issue of men's involvement as fathers and parents had not yet appeared prominently on the developing country women's agenda.

Immunization rates in Africa could never have reached the heights they did without the support of thousands of ordinary village and slum-dwelling women mobilizing around benefits for their children. In the best feminist sense it was their choice to do it through organization, effective leadership, and a renewed sense of power and capacity. The women NGOs active in this drive had other programmes for women's empowerment and could therefore easily incorporate children's concerns into their overall activities. Jim may not have noted the nuance, since it was women programme officers in countries working with women NGOs and progressively oriented government units that facilitated the dual approach. But the outcomes he saw vindicated his conviction that child survival and development could be achieved quickly and effectively if women took the lead.

The Nairobi Conference, then, reinforced the observation that for Jim Grant, the priorities of child survival and development overshadowed all other concerns, no matter how worthy. This applied not only to women's issues but pertained also to particular sets of children. Nothing should distract UNICEF from addressing the majority of those in need. Thus, he never really enthusiastically supported programmes focusing on children in especially difficult circumstances such as street children and abused children or urban basic services. Even child rights were marginalized until NGO pressures made him realize the power of civil society support. He shied away from taking the lead in emergency efforts, certain that these would drain on staff efforts and draw world attention from the majority of children in 'silent emergencies'.

Child survival and development programmes were becoming more clearly defined, objectives set and monitored, and representatives and regional directors held accountable for country performance. When the recession of the 1980s set in, and prospects for donor funding began to decline, Jim's strategy of focusing on doable actions worked. Donors allocated funds to UNICEF because they could see results in these essentially vertical programmes. Criticized as he was for oversimplifying approaches to child, Grant derived great satisfaction from seeing immunization rates rise to 95 per cent and more in several countries, even in war torn Uganda and beleaguered cities like Maputo in Mozambique.

The next headquarters Senior Policy Specialist on Women succeeding Nadia Youssef was anthropologist Agnes Aidoo. An expert on African development and women, Agnes initially found headquarters a difficult nut to crack. Almost total attention was going to child survival and development and related goals; women's concerns received low priority in New York's thinking. Not until she seized upon the girl child as her programme focus did she manage to make the link between women and child survival.

The priority given to the girl child beginning in the early nineties expressly aimed at reducing gender equalities, and monitored girls' status and needs. South Asia, the Middle East and North Africa, where discrepancies were most marked, took strongly to this approach, and Eastern and Southern Africa followed soon after. Special attention was given to the health, nutrition and education of young and adolescent girls. Within two years, these concerns were appearing in legislation and programmes that aimed at the reduction of early marriage and adolescent pregnancy. The concomitant drive to implement the Convention on the Rights of the Child and the goals of the World Summit for Children, with some of the goals focused specifically on girls and women, all reinforced UNICEF's focus on the girl child.

Working with Jim Grant in Africa

When Jim told me of his intention to appoint me the Regional Director for East Africa. I was speechless!

Once I had composed myself, I expressed great appreciation for his confidence in me. But, I added, my professional experience came mainly from Asia; I knew little about Africa beyond a few brief visits to UNICEF country offices there. Nor had I ever been a country representative. Moreover, although I had headed a university research institute in the Philippines, the largest the staff component had ever been was 120, with the norm at 50. As for financial management, my institute's budget had been minuscule compared to that of any UNICEF field office.

'Don't worry about the admin-finance part,' he countered. 'The office has skilled accountants and managers who take care of all that. Once I appoint you, the system will support you. You'll see. I want you in Nairobi because of your anthropology and social science background. The Regional Director has to have vision and a good understanding of culture, social change and the socio-cultural forces affecting Africa societies.'

He continued, citing my familiarity with development issues, my leadership abilities, and his determination to have more women in higher positions. Still overwhelmed by the offer, I mentioned my 83 year-old father, who was living with me in New York. What would I do about him? 'Is he healthy?' he countered.'Yes,' I replied. 'Then take him with you to Nairobi. It's a beautiful place.' Later that evening when I quoted Jim's exhortation to my father, the latter responded, 'Let's go!' and I accepted the position the very next day.

Some years later in passing, when Jim was especially pleased at something I had done, he said, 'And to think they called my appointing you 'Grant's folly'!' Whether the charge came from my never having been a representative, or my limited years in UNICEF, or some other reason, I shall never know. Cynics pointed to a pattern of Global Staff Association chairpersons being suddenly promoted to a field office when they became too successful at pushing staff concerns. Whatever the reason, I realized that he had taken a risk selecting me, and I was grateful. His decision opened up for me the exciting and rewarding experience of living and working in Africa.

Being a regional director placed you in a position of power. Although at the time, neither counterparts in other regions nor I directly supervised our respective representatives, we could exert two forms of authority over them.

Representatives had to obtain the regional director's permission to leave the country duty station. We also wrote their performance evaluation reports. Our regular presence was expected in New York, including at the Executive Board meetings. We participated in policy discussions, defined new programme directions, recommended people for posts, and had access to a wide range of information not readily available to most staff, even representatives. Moreover, the representative had a better chance of seeing the president or prime minister of the country in which she or he worked if accompanied by the regional director. For the women's network, having a woman advocate as regional director brought high expectations for heightened attention to gender in programmes and policies.

Their expectations were borne out. I monitored closely recruitment and promotion in the region, giving strong support to women and Africans, who remained disproportionately under represented on their own continent. My assessment that activities to benefit African women had to figure more strongly in UNICEF country programmes resulted in the Eastern and Southern Africa Regions (ESARO) making a concerted effort to take forward the economic directions approved at the Board. Mizrak Elias, whose extensive experience in business training and employment for women in Tanzania made her an ideal addition to the regional advisers team, developed a new framework for women's empowerment. Her skills went beyond advocacy to practical approaches for training poor women in mainstream enterprise development. Into this she incorporated women's status and rights issues. This commitment to their empowerment in turn implied programming with, rather than for, women. As the push for child rights gained ground in UNICEF, the argument in favour of women's rights as intrinsic to programmes moved forward.

Misrak established a network of programme officers whose skills in programming gender benefits increased enormously after a series of meetings and training sessions on the subject. Highlighted were the differences between a welfare and an empowerment orientation. When Safe Motherhood was jointly proclaimed as an important new strategy by several UN agencies – initially without UNICEF – she insisted it had to embody women's status, too. Women had to be at the centre – making decisions in their own interest. In Africa, these invariably covered children and family, and extended to community and society.

By 1991, in line with global trends, the term 'gender' was firmly entrenched in UNICEF discourse, emphasizing the importance of power relations between women and men. Moreover, the issue was no longer whether to programme for and with women. It was now a matter of how to do it. The region's training and networking activities helped answer that question, and Jim strongly approved. So long as representatives moved their countries rapidly toward the achievement of the goals of the Child Survival and Development Revolution, which had now been appropriated as World Summit goals, they could do anything else they wanted within the Board mandates. Realistically, however, child survival and development claimed almost 85 per cent of the total budget in 1992, leaving little for other programme concerns including women. Nonetheless, some creative staff managed to get women's concerns funded by tucking them into child survival and development activities.

Building on the participatory orientation of my predecessor, Karl-Eric Knutsson, I sustained his initiative of forming the representatives into a Regional Management Team. Those with more authoritarian tendencies could not believe I was serious about getting a collegial and participatory decision making process underway. They were used to regional directors who clung to power and insisted on exerting authority over the representative and country office staff. In my view, power came from the confidence one's staff had in their leader's commitment to listening to them and taking their proposals seriously. This collegial decision making in turn would unleash participants' creativity and encourage them to go all out in collaborating with their team members and contribute substantially to the planned outcome.

My insistence on recruiting many more women representatives meant heightened advocacy at the Regional Management Team for implementing the gender empowerment framework. At meeting after meeting, the representatives' confidence in this consensus building process had to be nurtured, negotiated and won. Jim liked this approach because it corresponded with his own set of principles and because it brought results. As always, however, the bottom line for him was, would this management style accelerate child survival and development? What did the GOBI-FFF indicators show?

Soon, ESARO's Regional Management Team (RMT) became the RPMT, to include planning. Representatives were no longer merely to implement and manage regional concerns planned by someone else, but rather begin their involvement at the planning stage in an interactive process with headquarters. It has been a source of personal gratification that ESARO at that time acquired a reputation as the most innovative and dynamic region, and the most gender active one in UNICEF. The credit goes largely to the representatives and their staffs, many women among them, who responded brilliantly when given the opportunity to forge new initiatives. As they came to appreciate the excitement and rewards of participation, I urged them to adopt some of these mechanisms in their own country offices, so as to generate the same kind of energy and commitment. Women staff were to receive particular attention and support. I was rarely disappointed.

Reeling in presidents and prime ministers

Over my nine years as ESARO Regional Director, I came to appreciate Jim Grant more and more. Accompanying him to call on a president or prime minister proved to be a fascinating learning exercise. He would list in a small notebook in his shirt pocket some five points that he expected to raise. The representative and regional director had to be prepared to furnish him with key information – how many children under five die per day in that country? This information would be transformed into the equivalent number of Boeing 757s filled to capacity crashing each day in that country. What are the immunization rates this year compared to last year? How many mothers use oral rehydration salts when their children suffer from diarrhoea? Are growth cards in common use? What proportion of children have growth cards?

Armed with this information, he would start his fishing expedition. After greeting the president or prime minister in a hearty and friendly manner and commenting on some interesting observation he had about the country, he would make his pitch. Had Jim not gone into development work, he could have become a millionaire with his super-salesman skills. Casting out the first line of conversation, he would assess whether the president was going to bite. If the latter showed only mild, courteous interest, out would come the next line, with the lure in the form of his famous visual aids. There was the tried and true packet of oral rehydration salts, or the restaurant matchbook with child survival messages on the igniting side. If this second line of conversation sparked an interest – Jim was skilled at reading people's faces and body language – he would firm up the line and gradually reel in the big fish. The process would never cease to amaze me.

What the president and his protocol officer assumed would be only a half hour courtesy visit would soon turn into an hour long working session. The president would at some point promise to devote quarterly cabinet meetings to reviewing progress in child immunization. Or, the prime minister would agree to speak with five other especially influential presidents and prime ministers at the next Organization for African Unity meeting to ensure that appropriate wording on oral rehydration use would go into their final resolutions. Sometimes he would even get across messages on women as defenders of children. From him I learned that visiting dignitaries calls for taking advantage of the opportunity to promote some kind of desired action, and not settle merely for polite, diplomatic talk.

Bringing in other partners

It was a privilege to work with Jim Grant on promoting child survival and development in Africa. I was with him in Mali when he conceptualized the Bamako Initiative with WHO Africa Regional Director, Gottfried Lobe Monekosso. The three of us then tackled WHO Executive Director, Halfden Mahler, who agreed to collaborate with UNICEF in this joint community financing for health initiative.

I accompanied Jim on many a hectic visit: to southern Sudan as part of Operation Lifeline to convince leaders of the southern liberation movements to bring immunization and other benefits to their children; to Ethiopia asking President Mengistu to open up a corridor of peace through his western border; to Japan to raise funds for child feeding, immunization and a million blankets for Ethiopians facing starvation; to a Angolan refugee camp in rebel territory to assess and respond to the situation of children there; to several OAU conferences where he persuaded African leaders to take on Summit goals for children; to Nigeria in search of breakthroughs in food production starting with cassava; to Uganda to learn about the emerging HIV/AIDS threat at a government hospital overflowing with cases; and to participate in triumphant celebrations all over Africa, featuring famous singers, dance troupes, and skilled drummers heralding the inauguration or achievement of immunization for their children.

These trips brought out his indefatigable drive and persuasive arguments to change the situation of children and challenge the conscience of governments about their most vulnerable citizens. Officials usually responded warmly, greatly admiring his zeal, charm and dedication. In one African country, for example, officials watched with both astonishment and amusement when, on a village visit, Jim noticed a large group of Chinese construction workers pausing from their tasks to watch the entourage go by. Like a long lost brother, he rushed over to greet them – in Chinese! Vigorously shaking hands with each of them, he elicited excited responses and flashing smiles from the

Chinese workers as he engaged them in animated conversation. Francophone officials who had earlier grumbled at his inability to speak French gained a new respect for his language abilities.

It was this human touch that conditioned many government leaders' reactions to Jim Grant. While the prospect of obtaining additional UNICEF assistance surely figured in their positive orientations, I truly believe that they welcomed and carried out his suggestions for more than that. First, these were doable. Second, he explained what they could accomplish and how, appealing to their pride and national self interest around children. And third, Jim Grant was such a likeable person.

The push for immunization and other child survival initiatives continued unabated in the early 1990s. Faltering programmes were allocated additional funds, and representatives sensed the implicit reprimand if their progress remained slow. Increased conflicts and warfare in the region and the early signs of the HIV/AIDS epidemic gave serious cause for concern, but we soldiered on. The converging enthusiasm of feminists and women and children advocates around the girl child brought positive results, even though they did lead to a de-emphasis on economic activities for women.

By the time the World Summit for Children took place in New York, millions of African children had been immunized under some of the most difficult conditions imaginable. Other aspects of child survival and development were also moving in various countries. This was a tribute to Jim Grant's conviction that the Child Survival and Development Revolution was doable, so long as everyone, especially women, mobilized around those goals. UNICEF's role was to continue calling attention to children's needs and effective ways of addressing them so that societies could fulfill their promises to children.

Jim was a man in a hurry. When after the death in 1988 of his first wife, Ethel, he married Ellan Young, he told me he was soon going to bring her with him to Africa. *'Will you do me a favour?'* he asked. Would I make sure, he continued, to arrange a really good photographic tour itinerary for Ellan in Kenya and possibly neighboring countries, while he was visiting local digni-taries? He wanted her to have the opportunity to understand and appreciate his efforts for children in developing countries, and link up her own work as a professional photographer with his. Perhaps concerned that his staff would think he was marrying too soon after Ethel's death, he added, quite out of the blue, that he did not really have the time for an extended courtship. As in everything he valued, he wanted her to be part of his mission as quickly as possible. They had to move fast ahead together in partnership. His personal message carried the same kind of urgency he brought to UNICEF: time was short and needs great. Everyone needed to move, and move fast.

Conclusion

Jim Grant envisioned women as selfless and inherently eager to be in the vanguard of initiatives on behalf of children. While UNICEF women saw that as instrumental, he interpreted it as women becoming crusading activists. To him, there was no contradiction. In a sense he was vindicated by the women who mobilized for child immunization throughout the developing world. There, women's groups supported the programme enthusiastically. Sustainability came for the most part through other programmes that addressed women's development, empowerment, status and rights.

Jim had no hesitation about asserting women's rights, and extolling sincerely their expanded economic and political roles along with the home-centred ones. In his single-minded drive to reach children, he supported virtually any strategy that worked for children. If women's empowerment was one of them, then by all means develop programmes to promote it. Assessing his pragmatic, results-oriented action for children, which also strongly incor-porated support to women, and setting aside the issue of how he conceptualized the issues, one would have to conclude that he was a indeed a great crusader for women – as women and as mothers.

Jim Grant loved his job. On a flight to Uganda, the UNICEF Representative Sally Fegan-Wyles and I were discussing with him exciting new possibilities in that country. Jim exclaimed with his characteristic enthusiasm, *'You know, I must have the best job in the world!'* Sally immediately countered, *'Oh no, Mr. Grant, the job of the UNICEF Representative is definitely the best job in the world.'* And she went on to explain why. I then chimed in with, *'You're both wrong. Being the UNICEF Regional Director is the best job in the world! I'm close to country developments but can take a broad regional perspective; yet I don't have the formidable fundraising responsibilities of the Executive Director. I have the best aspects of both your jobs plus my own!'*

The three of us looked at one another and laughed heartily. In what other organization in the world could such a debate have taken place? How many people love their job and their organization as much as we did? Jim Grant made UNICEF that kind of organization.

EXECUTIVE DIRECTOR

Ten commandments of Jim Grant's leadership for development

by Kul Gautam

Adapted from a statement delivered at the International Development Conference, Washington DC, 13 January 1997.

The late James P. Grant, former Executive Director of UNICEF, was a visionary with a missionary zeal. I have never encountered a man, or a woman, whose faith in human capacity for doing good was so profound, and whose capacity for seeing a silver lining in every dark cloud was so total. A man of holistic vision, Grant was very aware of the great complexities of development issues. But he was a great master at simplifying complex issues until they became easily understandable and readily doable.

Grant believed that more human progress has been made in this century than in all previous human history. It was not the dramatic decline in infant mortality, increase in life expectancy or reduction of illiteracy that were the key indicators of this human progress. The most significant trans- formation in human development, he believed, was the fact that for the first time in history, we regard it as normal that the world order should be organized for the benefit of the teeming masses rather than for the benefit of the chosen few.

Grant often quoted Arnold Toynbee, who said that *'the twentieth century will be chiefly remembered in future centuries not as an age of political conflicts or technical inventions, but as an age in which human society dared to think of the welfare of the whole human race as a practical objective.'* Grant devoted half a century of his own professional life to pursuing this objective. Arguing that morality must march in step with the growing capacity of governments, international agencies, NGOs and civil society, he tirelessly advocated for universal access to basic services. He used the resources and the bully pulpit as the head of UNICEF to influence policies and priorities of governments, international agencies, NGOs and others in a crusade that is credited with saving the lives of some 25 million children, improving the health and well-being of millions more and contributing to a people-centred ethics of development.

What strategies did Grant employ to achieve such remarkable results? And what lessons can be learned from his approach to development? Some have argued that Grant was a one-of-a-kind phenomenon. I believe that, while he was in a class of his own in his indefatigable optimism and can-do spirit, the strategies he followed are readily replicable in the hands of leaders with a vision and genuine commitment to development. In fact, these strategies are being applied today in many countries, communities and organizations throughout the world with good results.

In his last *State of the World's Children Report* in 1995 Grant summarized the strategies that he had found particularly effective in his promotion of the Child Survival and Development Revolution and the follow up to the World Summit for Children. Drawing on these and other attempts to distill lessons of his leadership, I would group Grant's strategy for accelerating human development under what I would refer to as the 'Ten Commandments' of Jim Grant's leadership for development.

1. Articulate your vision for development in terms of inspiring goals

Grant believed in the mobilizing power of measurable goals. Fuzzily formulated general aims of development tend to be a prescription for evasion and non-accountability. Broad development objectives such as 'Sustainable Development' or 'Health for All' or 'Education for All' sum up a desired end result, but give no clue as to how to get there. Such broad aims need to be transformed into more concrete goals such as reducing infant mortality by a certain percentage, increasing adult literacy rates to a certain level or eradicating a dreaded disease from the face of the earth, all of which can help achieve the broad objectives of development.

2. Break down goals into time-bound, doable propositions

Even concrete national or international goals need to be translated into specific actions that can be taken at the sub-national, community or family level. Often this means setting proxy goals and intermediate targets. Sometimes it requires a sub-goal of mobilizing the means or creating the precondition for achieving the larger goal. Most importantly, goals should be broken down to actionable propositions within the lifetime of today's political leadership, before the next election or the next *coup d'état*.

Goals can be very powerful means for mobilizing action, for ensuring accountability of public officials and for enhancing the efficiency and effectiveness of service delivery systems. But a goal-oriented approach also has its downside. It can lead to too much attention on the end results, and neglect of participatory processes. It can distort priorities by emphasizing the measurable versus the truly important. It can lead to imposition of national or even global goals on reluctant local communities. And it can corrupt the development process by giving disproportionate attention to programmes for which funding is readily available from governments and donors.

Indeed misuse of goals and targets in some countries, especially in family planning programmes, has led to a general antipathy towards a goal-oriented approach to development in some circles. But it would be 'throwing the baby out with the bath water' not to capitalize on the enormous power and potential of a goal-oriented approach. There are ways in which goals can be selected and pursued that command universal acceptance. Pitfalls of goals can be minimized. We can adopt goals that empower people, and avoid those that victimize them. We all ought to be for goals that inspire people, not intimidate them; goals that challenge us, not frighten us; goals that are ambitious but achievable. In this post-cold war era what we need are goals that are equivalent in excitement to the 'man in the moon', not cynical protestations of 'dog in the manger'.

In the 'lost decade' of development in the 1980s, Jim Grant led a movement that, with carefully crafted goals and strategies, brought about a child survival revolution against great odds. It showed that under dynamic leadership the United Nations system can make a great difference. It vindicated a creative, goal-oriented approach to development.

3. Demystify techniques and technologies

Many development programmes are expressed in such technical terms as to be understood only by specialists. For any programme to develop a large following, it is vital to communicate the required actions and techniques in the simplest possible terms. Presented or demonstrated in ways that voters and politicians can understand, large scale actions develop their own constituencies of concerned citizens and activists. The ubiquitous packet or oral rehydration salts (ORS) that Jim Grant waved, and the way in which he encouraged presidents, prime ministers, governors and mayors to personally administer polio vaccines or test iodized salt, left a lasting impression of the practicality of these interventions. Far too many technocrats and bureaucrats alienate the very people whom they are trying to help by failing to communicate in a language they can understand. Instead of being their best allies, people become passive bystanders when development-speak characterizes action for development. Demystifying the techniques of development is therefore essential for ensuring popular participation, ownership and empowerment of participants and beneficiaries of development programmes.

4. Generate and sustain political commitment

Quite often social development programmes are the domains of weak and under-funded ministries, vulnerable to budget cuts in times of austerity. Securing the commitment of top political leadership, at national as well as provincial and local levels, and the commitment of departments that control resource allocation is vital. But this requires convincing these leaders that it is in their political interest to identify themselves with success in pursuing such development goals. Once secured, political commitment must be sustained, and reaffirmed whenever there is a change in government or leadership. Fostering a national consensus on human development goals helps ensure that such goals do not become vulnerable to changes in political winds. Grant was able to mobilize the political commitment of a wide spectrum of leaders – democrats and dictators – for the well-being of children. The World Summit for Children, the largest gathering of world leaders until that time, was of course the pinnacle of his achievement. But there are scores of other examples showing that when political will is cultivated, resources can be found even when budgets are tight.

5. Mobilize a grand alliance of all social forces

Even the best run government ministries cannot reach all people. But with today's information and communications capacity, it is possible to mobilize a vast array of actors for promoting development. Once sectoral straight-jackets are thrown off, many development programmes can be turned into movements around which 'grand alliances' can be built involving the media and the NGOs, the churches and the school children, private marketing channels and public policy forums.This is how Jim Grant turned what might have been a conventional programme of technical assistance into a movement for child survival and development. And as a builder of movements, Grant was genuinely generous in giving credit to all partners, big and small, whose contribution made a difference.

6. Go to scale

The development map of the world is littered with pilot studies and demonstration projects. Some of these have been useful for innovation and replication, but far too many have been more beneficial to local officials, researchers and donors than to the intended beneficiaries. Few develop-ment programmes attempt to take action on a scale commensurate with the problems they are trying to tackle. Grant was convinced that going to scale with a few ambitious but achievable actions was extremely important, both on its own merit and as a powerful boost for broader development advocacy. Against all odds, and often the derision of conventional devel-opment experts and academics, Grant advocated that immunization levels be raised from 10 per cent to 80 per cent within a few years; that the world's major cause of mental retardation be tamed by iodizing all of the world's salt; that major strides be made in reducing illiteracy; universalizing access to primary education; and expanding the availability of safe drinking water and sanitation. Dramatic achievements were registered in each of these areas, and many more. The lives of over 3 million children a year are being saved today because immunization programmes went to scale. One and a half billion more people are consuming iodized salt today than at the beginning of the 1990s because of the effort to iodize salt on a scale commensurate with the magnitude of its deficiency. Net primary school enrolment rose from 50 per cent to 80 per cent in the 1980s with significant reductions in gender disparities. Over a billion people got access to safe water supply in the decade of the 1980s. While the remaining problems are still staggering, the record of achievement in human development is an impressive one.

7. Select your priorities and stick to them

Many development agencies suffer from trying to do too many things, often in a mediocre manner rather than doing a few important things, and doing them well. One of the great strengths of Jim Grant was his ability to select just a few priorities and stick to them. This is easier said than done. For someone of Grant's broad vision of development, and can-do spirit, there were always many temptations to become involved in many issues. The needs of children are many and the constituencies clamouring for UNICEF's attention are manifold. But Grant led UNICEF to devote a lion's share of its resources and efforts to just a few major interventions – immunization and oral rehydration therapy among them. He withstood the criticism about being tunnel visioned, and never tired of advocating for his priorities. The results have been spectacular: during the 1990s guinea worm disease, which had affected over a million people in Africa, was reduced by 90 per cent; deaths due to measles were reduced by 85 per cent; the reported cases of polio were reduced by 99 per cent and eliminated in at least 110 countries; one and a half million child deaths were averted every year by popularizing the low-cost, low-tech oral rehydration therapy; the eye sight and nutritional status of millions of children were protected by vitamin A supplementation; and over 90 million children are being protected every year from learning disability thanks to dramatic progress in salt iodization. Grant could have taken the easy path of doing many miscellaneous good things for children in a small scale. That would have certainly satisfied a larger number of constituencies clamouring for UNICEF's attention, but it would probably have left a legacy of great underachievement for UNICEF, a sad characteristic of too many UN agencies.

8. Institute public monitoring and accountability

The beauty of measurable goals is that progress can be regularly monitored. But to use it effectively to accelerate progress or to take corrective actions, monitoring must not be confined to specialized expert analysis. It must involve and inform political leaders and the media, NGO activists and the participating communities. Publicizing the progress and retrogression, using indicators that the public can understand, is essential for maximum benefit of a goal-oriented programme. Generating healthy competition by comparing the performance of neighbouring districts or neighbouring countries is often a great catalyst for faster progress. UNICEF's annual report, *The Progress of Nations*, contributed to such monitoring at the global level on progress towards the goals adopted at the World Summit for Children. A major challenge in monitoring social development programmes is that relevant statistics are not collected, processed or disseminated with sufficient frequency. Grant pressed his staff and others to give priority to the compilation of social statistics in the same timely manner as some of the common economic data. Methodologies for doing so, including the multiple indicator cluster surveys, were devised and widely used. This made the World Summit for Children the most systematically followed up and rigorously monitored of all major UN conferences and summits of the 1990s.

9. Ensure relevance to broader development agenda

A corollary to being selective and focused is not to lose sight of the broader context of development. Grant's interest in development was very broad, multi-faceted and holistic. His keen sense of strategy led him to work on several high profile success stories lending him credibility to push for even more ambitious goals. But he always saw the child survival and development actions he promoted so vigorously as a springboard for sustainable human development. In his annual *State of the World's Children Report* Grant boldly addressed issues ranging from the need for reducing military expenditures, to providing debt relief for developing countries, promoting adjustment with a human face, ending the apartheid of gender and restructuring aid and national budgets in favour of basic social services. Grant believed that success in ambitious programmes for children and women could be the Trojan Horse for attacking the citadel of poverty, for undergirding democracy, dramatically slowing population growth and for accelerating economic development.

10. Unleash the full potential of the United Nations system

Grant was a true believer in the principles of the United Nations and its great – if under used – potential for promoting peace and development. While some viewed the series of major UN conferences of the 1970s and 1990s as futile and unproductive, Grant saw them as developing consensus and commitment for the great issues of our times: environment, population, shelter, health, food and nutrition, education, human rights, social development and women's empowerment. There was an in-house joke in UNICEF that Grant never saw a Summit that he did not like. A more apt rendering would be that he never went to a Summit from which he did not win a significant commitment for children. He was masterful in exploiting the potential of the UN system: in mobilizing sister agencies to help accelerate action for children, in influencing other agencies' policies and priorities, in finding common ground and forging solidarity among agencies, and by offering, without being pretentious, a personal model of vision and leadership. The World Summit for Children was a crowning achievement of his career both in terms of how he used the UN system so effectively to fashion an inspiring agenda for children and development with ambitious but practical goals, and a vigorous follow up with impressive results.

Today we see much cynicism and pessimism about development cooperation. Instead of the end of cold war generating a peace dividend and a new momentum for development, we see the growth of a mean spirit of inward looking, isolationist impulses in many countries. Although our nightly news tends to be dominated by stories of failures of development, the fact is that the daily lives of three-quarters of humanity are now characterized by unprecedented progress and success stories of development. To recapture the excitement for development cooperation we need the can-do, must-do spirit so characteristic of Jim Grant. He helped us to lift our gaze from today's depressing headlines to tomorrow's exciting horizons.

Raising the United Nations flag on a relief truck during 'Operation Lifeline Sudan', 1989.

Explaining the challenge of the World Summit for Children, September 1990.

Completing Jim Grant's 'Agenda for the World's Children'

by Jon Rohde

Adapted from the James P. Grant Memorial Address presented at the Global Health Council's 27th Annual Conference, Arlington, Virginia, USA, 14 June 2000.

The UN Special Session on Children comes eleven years after the first ever summit of world leaders, the World Summit for Children. That unique gathering was a culmination of James Grant's dream that the world would stop for a moment to make a commitment to care for its young.

That same month in 1990, the Convention on the Rights of the Child was ratified by the twentieth nation, making it international law. It is now ratified by all the nations of the world, save two. It is important to recognize the momentousness of this fact. The Convention on the Rights of the Child is virtually the only universal law of this earth. There is consensus that its provisions represent the finest aspirations of each of us. The declaration of the World Summit for Children, with its precise agenda for the decade of the '90s, defined what the Convention on the Rights of the Child means for children in specific, practical terms.

During the three days of the UN Special Session on Children, world leaders will seek to analyse both our successes and our failures in order to better understand why in many cases we have failed, and how we can do better in the future to realize the promises that we have made. Jim would surely have begun the process of shared analysis and understanding with a few observations along the following lines:

First, how have we done?

We have had successes. We followed up the World Summit for Children with a push on polio. True, the virus has not been eradicated – yet. But annual cases have been reduced from nearly 400,000 in 1990 to fewer than 2,000 in 2000. Guinea worm, too, is all but eradicated. Salt is now iodized in most countries, preventing millions of cases of mental impairment. And millions more people now have access to drinkable water. More kids are in schools, especially girls. Thanks largely to the Cairo Summit, family planning is used by more couples than ever before.

But is such progress being sustained?

Jim Grant drove all countries to formulate a national plan of action to put substance to promises made. This brought real enthusiasm and momentum until mid-decade, by which time the intermediate goals had been substantially achieved. Then, in early 1995, Jim left us. And the momentum faded.

Today, we face the fact that in much of the world Jim's dream too is fading. The great drive to meet the most pressing needs of millions of the world's poorest children is losing momentum, running out of steam. Immunization coverage has fallen in most countries from the 80 per cent level that was achieved across much of the world. In some countries, the level today is below 50 per cent again. And it is estimated that over 25 million children born last year are not yet protected. While more children are in school, 130 million are not – 60 per cent of them girls. Even Jim's favourite ORT (oral rehydration therapy) is used in less than half the cases of diarrhoea. In India, after 30 years of promotion, ORT is used in only about one fifth of episodes of diarrhoeal disease. Overall, the infant mortality rate that had been falling steadily over recent decades has now plateaued in many countries. In India it has stagnated at 70 per 1,000 live births. In many African countries it is rising, often in association with the AIDS epidemic.

The most alarming fact about the world's children is that even now, at the beginning of the new millennium, a quarter of a million under-fives die every week from disease and malnutrition. No famine, no flood, no drought, no earthquake has ever killed a quarter of a million children in a single week. Yet the 'silent emergency' of ordinary malnutrition and disease continues to claim that number *every week*. Many millions more live on with ill health, poor growth, and perhaps worst of all, stunted mental development. It is unacceptable for this tragedy to continue, precisely because we have the means to prevent it. Jim constantly reminded us that morality must march with capacity. That we have the capacity is not in doubt. And not to act at this time is to tacitly acquiesce in the verdict of a world which says that these children do not matter because they are the sons and daughters of the poorest people on earth. Why have we not done better? What happened to Jim's 'revolution' for children?

It is poverty, say so many. All is the result of poverty. We cannot redress this failure until we eliminate the poverty that is everywhere and so profound. Is this true? Nobel laureate economist Amartya Sen has long insisted that poverty is not really about income, not even about economics. He says poverty is about *'freedoms from'* – freedom from premature death, freedom from illness, freedom from hunger, from ignorance, from exploitation, freedom from violence. Precisely Jim's point: there are many poverties – including hunger, ignorance, and vulnerability. And the worst thing about being poor is not lack of money, but lack of survival.

It has been argued that the World Summit for Children goals address only the symptoms of poverty and leave the causes undisturbed. Jim saw this as an unacceptable argument on two counts. First, it is an inhuman argument. How much longer must the poorest families wait? When will we decide that the world has reached the level of economic development at which a few dollars per capita can be afforded to help prevent millions of the children of the poor from becoming malnourished, blinded, crippled, mentally retarded, dead? Second, it fails to recognize that frequent illness, malnutrition, poor growth, and illiteracy are some of the most fundamental causes, as well as some of the most severe symptoms, of income poverty. The World Summit for Children clearly identified the things that can and should be done to eliminate these worst poverties, without waiting for economic development.

Perhaps cost has prevented us from doing more. But the summit declaration itself declared: *'the financial resources required are modest....'* And the World Bank Development Report in 1993 showed that essential health care can cost as little as $14 per person per year in low income countries. Education for all is a reality for several million poor kids in Bangladesh in BRAC schools for only $21 per pupil per year. To provide safe water supply requires an investment of only some $10 to15 per person. Article four of the Convention on the Rights of the Child obligates each country to *'undertake such measures to the maximum extent of their available resources'* and obligates the international community to help. Do we really believe the world cannot afford these modest investments?

The amount given in overseas development assistance for nutrition, primary health care, water and sanitation, primary education, and family planning comes to about $4 billion a year. Jim would chide us, pointing out that this is less than half the sum the aid-giving nations spend each year on sports shoes or a quarter of what the US pays for pet food.

Is it that more fortunate people round the world just don't care? It certainly would seem so, when viewed from the perspective of government spending for overseas development assistance. It is at an all time low – only one tenth of one per cent of GDP in the world's richest country. Could it be that, as some become more and more wealthy, as the gap between the rich and the desperately deprived yawns wider, the rich become more and more protective, more selfish, and turn inward? Can we not rekindle human compassion as a global society? And be the richer for it? Jim Grant would be cajoling us, for our own sakes, as well as for the sake of the world's children.

People invariably respond to the distress of a single child. Look at the appeals for help in disasters and emergencies. Again and again people donate, wanting to help those in need. The successes of non-governmental organizations, many represented at the UN Special Session, are based on the public confidence that they reach individual children in need, that they provide a chance for people to reach out to other, less fortunate people. Rotary has raised over $320 million for polio eradication, having set an ambitious goal of $100 million, a goal that was surpassed in the early years of the campaign; and the money continues to pour in. Many government-aided bilateral programmes, and those of the United Nations, are well conceived and effectively implemented. Jim would be reminding everyone of those success stories, baiting national pride with tales of neighbouring accomplishments. He was a master of the strategic anecdote, bringing a 'can be done' story to every discussion. Do each nation's taxpayers realize how well their money is spent for children? Success breeds success and people everywhere dig deeper into pockets in support of successful actions for children. That is how Jim raised UNICEF's annual budget to over 1 billion dollars. Citizens are generous when the idea is precise, the technology available and robust, and the vision clear and noble. We need Jim's story telling skills – simple, enthusiastic, visionary – so that citizens will demand their governments show similar generosity.

The real problem today is that we have lost our vision and the commitment and enthusiasm that vision engenders. Resignation and cynicism are always self-fulfilling prophecies. *'Perhaps,'* Jim said, *'being involved in a cause larger than oneself is a deep human need from which we have been diverted by the particular direction that development has taken in recent times.'* The Convention on the Rights of the Child could provide that vision, but it needs a visionary to give it life - its 54 articles are too legalistic, too formal. They lack life; they lack children! Jim Grant translated these articles into real, visible terms, and he made us each believe that we can accomplish goals if we concretize and believe in them – and believe in ourselves. He called on each of us to pause and think: to maintain our own optimism, daily we must envision the future and then strive throughout the day to achieve that vision. I saw Jim face every day with such renewal.

Often, in setting goals, we have obscured our own vision with averages. The World Summit for Children and other global gatherings have set laudable societal goals, invariably expressed as averages or national rates: reduced infant mortality rate, halving of malnutrition, increased school enrolment. It is time for us to measure not the averages, but the conditions prevailing amongst the lowest fifth or lowest third of society. What is their mortality, prevalence of malnutrition, participation in school?

India provides excellent examples: in rural areas 80 of each 1,000 infants die in the first year, while in urban areas the rate is about 40 per 1,000. But in the slums of Delhi, rarely measured and never mentioned, infant mortality exceeds 120 per 1,000. In the poorest districts, the rate exceeds 160 per 1,000 – twice the rural and four times the urban average. School enrolment in India is at last reaching 80 per cent or even 85 per cent, but amongst scheduled cast and tribal girls, literacy is still less than 20 per cent. And although the average prevalence of malnutrition is shockingly high at 50 per cent, in the poorest communities an adequately nourished child is an exception. Thousands of girls of poor families are forced into prostitution annually, millions of their children labour in slave-like conditions. Jim constantly reminded us that the true state of a society is measured by the state of its poor, not by averages.

But disparity is widespread and a source of discontent in all societies throughout the world. Indeed poverty is often relative, even when measured by lack of freedoms. The poor in the United States are defined by an income level that, even when adjusted for purchasing power, would be the envy of billions in Africa and Asia. They are poor only in comparison to those amidst whom they live. They suffer from inequality. Jim's view was that inequality and relative poverty would be the great challenges of the future, but that the great task of the present was to defeat absolute poverty – to put in place a safety net below which no one on earth should be allowed to fall. This is what bred Jim's preoccupation with 'survival' – surely not all there is to life, but an essential and inalienable first right.

And while he said it over and over, many did not hear Jim's assurances that survival is the *sine qua non* for everything else. *'Oh, but life is more than survival and more than GOBI,'* (the acronym Jim used for the key survival interventions of growth monitoring, oral rehydration therapy, breastfeeding, and immunisation). *'Development must be development in all its forms,'* said the well-meaning special interests who rushed to add their particular priorities. But sadly, these other priorities did little for the hundred million children who have died needlessly since that first World Summit – children who have died for lack of GOBI and related affordable interventions. Without survival, the rest is meaningless. The Convention on the Rights of the Child does say in article six, *'every child has the inherent right to life,'* a right enshrined in almost every national constitution, as well as in the Universal Declaration of Human Rights. There is a hierarchy, even within the moral minimum, and every time we choose to invest in something beyond survival we are making a vital choice. Jim knew this, and while he was never against any action for children, he kept his 'eye on the ball' – the essentials come first!

Recently, the plethora of studies on 'burden of disease' and 'disability adjusted life years', has diverted world attention to a whole new range of problems crying for resources. Usually, those problems include the concerns of the world's average citizen, the global majority, rather than those of the global poor. These studies have shown that, as people rise out of poverty, increasing numbers reach old age and suffer from the illnesses attendant thereon: chronic, degenerative conditions like heart disease and cancer, and mental conditions like neuroses and anxiety. In response to these 'average conditions', some experts now counsel shifts of resources toward the inevitable problems of ageing. Such shifts would increasingly leave the world's poor minority to cope on their own with the unfinished agenda of nutritional, perinatal, and communicable diseases, especially amongst children – the very conditions that deny survival to millions, yet are largely either preventable or susceptible to cheap interventions.

Nutrition is a prime example; iodine and vitamin A cost pennies, while deficits of these micronutrients have effects that last a lifetime. Jim saw these as affordable universal interventions that could and should reach every child on earth. By not guaranteeing adequate nutrition of today's infants, we not only reduce their mental potential and ensure that they will suffer higher prevalence of degenerative disease in late life, but we also ensure that their children will also suffer in the next generation. Bad ethics, worse economics!

By focusing on 'disability adjusted life years' we are confusing 'prevalence' of ill health with 'severity' of ill health – suggesting an equality in the importance of discomfort and ageing among the global majority on the one hand, and the fatal outcomes that afflict the world's poor minority, primarily children. In a recent paper for the World Bank, Davidson Gwatkin, a close colleague of Jim's in the Overseas Development Council, has shown how increased allocation of resources to the increasingly prevalent conditions of ageing would benefit all levels of society. From a global perspective, such allocation in this manner would seem to be a truly democratic choice, serving the majority. But by discriminating in favour of those fortunate enough to reach adulthood, poor-rich disparities in life expectancy would actually grow, inequity would increase, and more children would be left behind. The 'epidemiological polarization' resulting from the widely heralded demographic-epidemiological 'health transition' would be exacerbated.

We have failed, because we have not yet finished what we started under Jim Grant's leadership. It is too early to move on to other claims. The goals of the World Summit for Children are still valid, still the best buy, still the best formula for achieving equity. They represent the spirit and intent of the Convention on the Rights of the Child. Our failure to achieve these goals leaves several million children dead each year. Twenty five million infants born last year are not fully immunized, over a million of them will die. ORT is used in less than half of cases of diarrhoea – three million die. Vitamin A could prevent the death of one to two million more children. Breastfeeding continues to recede under attack from private sector marketing of infant formula. Old messages? Yes, they are! Like clean water to drink. Recently, the global water forum counselled us to consider water a consumer item, a desired product for sale rather than a right! Should our failure to deliver on essential rights lead us to dissipate our efforts into an even broader range of products and then turn them over to the private sector for sale? What then for the poor?

Jim Grant always said it is easy to start something new, but so much harder to stay the course. *'Nothing,'* he said, *'would have been easier than to come up with a new and catchy idea every year or two.'* The Child Survival and Development Revolution is still valid today and still needed to redress the worst poverties. We must finish what we started.

There have been calls for a 'rights approach' to national development – attractive in principle, but only if it avoids the pitfalls of diversification of our efforts. It must support, not diffuse, our collective vision for children. Rights may be universal but access to them is surely not. Only rights to which access can be achieved will change the lives of the poorest. Rights which can not be delivered are false promises – the stock-in-trade of duplicitous politicians, not development professionals. Only an approach which gives priority to the most fundamental rights of the most disadvantaged people will reduce the worst inequities. The 'rights approach' that Jim would propose is individualistic, one in which we give priority to our concern that every child, including the poorest, will have his or her basic needs addressed. Such a 'rights approach' is in direct contrast with the 'averages approach', which is so prone to hide or camouflage the problems of minority groups – the silent, the unseen, the poor.

For the decade ahead, I think Jim would give us five principles:

First; basic freedoms. The civil and political rights are fundamental. They are both an end in themselves, as well as a means to realizing social and economic rights, the 'aspirational rights' as some call them. Amartya Sen refers to the *'pre-eminence of political freedoms and democracy'* – the freedom to vote, of expression, to be heard – as being of direct importance in creating the political environment to prioritize and value the needs of the poor. More so, Jim would remind us, for children, who are rarely heard and never vote. With freedoms must come responsibility. Our responsibility to frame and implement effective programmes, and to inform the public of what can and should be done for children, is the only voice children have. Is it not also the responsibility of those who profit from global trade to accept a negligible taxation – say 0.1 per cent of transactions – to be used as a global fund for children? Recently, former President Nelson Mandela called for each nation to create a Ministry for Children in order to give political voice and resources directly to children. Without such actions, children will never be heard, will never know real freedom.

Second; we must defend children's right to survival and development with the same intensity with which we defend civil and political rights. Democracy is spreading across the world, bringing its benefits to the majority of citizens, regardless of rank or income. Where democracy prevails, children do better. Democracy, however, is not a magic bullet. Jim challenged us to organize programmes for the survival and development of children with the same thoroughness and resources that we now dedicate to elections. Let us defend the right of freedom to learn to read with the same ardour with which we defend freedom to write in the press. Let us protect children from forced prostitution and exploitative labour with the same energy with which we protect accused adults in a court of law. The basic rights of children must no longer take a back seat to the rights of their more articulate and politically active parents.

Third; democracy is fundamentally local. Only when management is decentralized to communities is effective action and accountability best assured. Jim Grant often claimed that the high infant mortality rate in Washington, DC, was a direct result of the disenfranchisement of its citizens; and he noted the fall in infant mortality in Puerto Rico that closely followed the introduction of self-government as evidence for the political accountability to social goals. During the past decade, the most successful programmes for children were designed and carried out by small groups of concerned people, working at the community level. Too rarely have governments found affordable ways to guarantee Sen's freedoms; more rarely still to ensure transparency and accountability. More commonly, NGOs and communities have found how to piece together complex, local solutions to development. Their success, however, in no way absolves government from its obligation to provide the needed resources from public revenues. But when it comes to implementation, children stand the best chance of realizing their rights when developmental resources are managed close to home. Jim often paraphrased Tip O'Neil's *'All politics are local'* with *'All actions for children are local.'*

Fourth; he would argue the need to measure and expose the situation of children, especially those deprived of their rights and freedoms. Monitoring should become more sensitive to disparity. It should focus less on averages and more on those who are being excluded – identifying who they are, where they are, and why they are being marginalized. Jim was an avid consumer of measurements, for with them he could see where attention was most needed. And he found measurement of disparity a major motivating tool which he used to great effect. His early work on the Physical Quality of Life Index and the Disparity Reduction Rate presaged the development of indices used widely today by the World Bank and UN agencies. With Peter Adamson he pioneered *The Progress of Nations'* annual ranking of countries as *'a contribution towards that day when nations will be judged ... by the protection that is afforded to the growing minds and bodies of their children.'*

Amartya Sen believes that one of democracy's direct benefits is the link it fosters between visibility – particularly the visibility which comes from the availability of data – and social action. Article 44 of the Convention on the Rights of the Child requires each state to report on the fulfilment of its obligations under the Convention, both to a UN committee of experts on child rights, and importantly, to the citizens of the state. Matters previously protected by notions of 'sovereignty' have been brought, by the Convention on the Rights of the Child, under international scrutiny and made everybody's business. Public exposure and effective use of the media is the strongest tool Jim left us.

Finally, we must ensure the honesty and transparency of our own efforts. To realize the full benefits of this new public honesty, the UN Committee, indeed each of us, must become more candid in our analysis. We must become less politically sensitive; less bound by diplomatic niceties. We must disseminate our findings more widely. We must treat states and societies equitably, even as we work for children's equity. The rights of children are too important to subordinate them to the relatively petty interests of the technical, economic, and political elite who manage public resources. In short, like Jim, we must speak out. Children's rights are now everybody's business and everybody's responsibility.

In conclusion, the UN Special Session on Children is called to celebrate and reaffirm the relevance and importance of the promises made to children by world leaders a decade ago. Those goals are still affordable. They still provide a clear guideline for national and international priorities. They indicate exactly what each of us want for our own children, our grandchildren. What we want for our own is what is fair and decent for all children. Rights are not averages. They apply to each child. They can be realized only by reaching each child. And, while jurists tell us all rights are equal, we must respect the obvious priority of survival. *'What do you want to be when you grow up?'* Jim Grant had asked Selema Wit, a little Ethiopian girl. *'Alive!'* she responded. Without it nothing else matters.

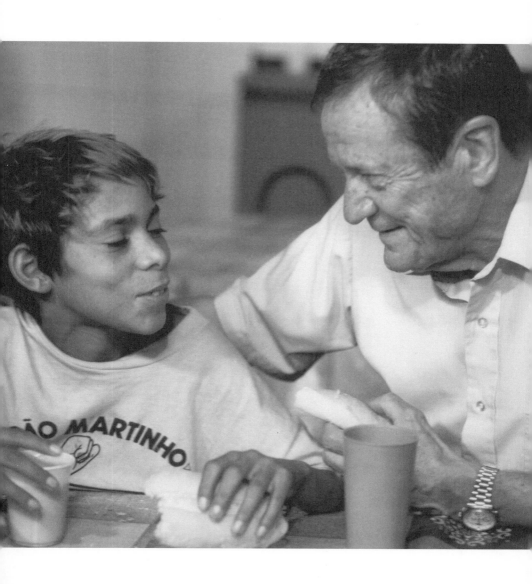

Jim Grant in his own words

Selections by Sheila Barry Tacon

We cannot allow

We cannot allow the largest generation of children ever to occupy the earth to grow up malnourished, unhealthy and uneducated in order to become the parents of another generation of malnourished, unhealthy and uneducated and more numerous children. Instead we must accord our children – and their future children – the priority that they deserve.

A significant improvement in the lives of children by the end of this century will certainly require a significant increase in resources and in the effectiveness of their deployment. Yet it is a question not of possibilities, but priorities, a matter of choice in which both reason and emotion argue for children. That is an argument that we in UNICEF and our colleagues in National Committees for UNICEF, and NGOs independently around the world, are determined to assert in every forum open to us.

UNICEF ANNUAL REPORT 1981

People's participation

If the potential importance of paraprofessional development workers is one of the 'legs' of a strategy of 'more development per dollar', then the concept of people's participation is the other. Indeed without the organized participation of the poor, no community development project has more than the dimmest hope of lasting success. If amid the scattered hopes of a failed development project, there was a little black box to record what had gone wrong, it would always turn out to be the case that, somewhere on the way, the people for whose benefit the project was intended had found better things to do with their time.

THE STATE OF THE WORLD'S CHILDREN REPORT 1981-82

Universal Child Immunization

We must remember in pursuing Universal Child Immunization by 1990, that while it is an end in itself, it is much more important as a means of accomplishing many other things. We must not get trapped into treating it as an end in itself. This is why we frequently refer to 'Universal Child Immunization by 1990 to the third power' since we really want to accomplish three objectives. One, we want children to be immunized. Two, it must be on a sustainable basis, and third it must be the door opener for other programmes – other GOBI (growth monitoring, oral rehydration therapy, breastfeeding, immunization) programmes, other primary health care programmes.

ADDRESS TO THE WARSAW COLLOQUIUM OF UNICEF NATIONAL COMMITTEES, WARSAW, 2 SEPTEMBER 1985

A sense of optimism

The Child Survival and Development Revolution is today making the kind of progress that warrants a sense of optimism – a conviction that something can be done to change the tragedies that we heretofore considered unchangeable. As people build their ability to take care of their families, and build their confidence in their personal capacity to do so, they strengthen their ability to build their communities … and their nations and to truly take control of their own future. The principles we are practicing, and the approaches that are being pioneered, are applicable for adult health as well as children's, and for new risks arising from traditional 'progress' as well as the historic scourges of old, not to mention a broad range of non-health areas in which true progress is long overdue.

THE MCBRIDE LECTURE, CASE WESTERN UNIVERSITY, CLEVELAND, 24 SEPTEMBER 1986

Adjustment with a human face

... in the great majority of countries – industrialized as well as developing – far too much emphasis remains, first on cure rather than prevention, and second, on excessive reliance on medical facilities for improving health to the neglect of schools, radio, television and other communication facilities which can transfer much of health prevention and care to the family. Even within the curative sector and despite the growing emphasis of recent decades on reaching the poorer majority, the more affluent minority still benefit disproportionately. Regretfully, in many countries the global recession has even further exacerbated this situation.

The challenge lies in moving from a consensus on principles for better adjustment practices to concrete actions. The adjustment process must be broadened so as to include a minimum floor for basic human needs; the health, education and social sectors must be restructured so as to meet these needs; and, in the broader scope, the economy must be restructured so as to emphasize employment policies and action which provide both increased output and more income for the disadvantaged.

DISCUSSION PAPER FOR THE SYMPOSIUM ON THE OPPORTUNITIES FOR AFRICAN INTELLECTUALS AND ARTISTS, DAKAR, 20–23 MARCH 1987

Prerequisite to progress

Breaking down grandiose plans of development into a series of specific and achievable goals is now a prerequisite to progress. We can break immunization down into a discreet and doable series of steps. We can break the control of diarrhoea and dehydration into discreet and actionable steps. Among the governments of the rich and the poor worlds it is the possibility of achievement which triggers commitment and releases resources, which in turn build confidence and raise expectations, which continue the progressive spiral by fueling further hopes and further efforts. If the first steps along that new path are virtually modest, the destination is among the grandest of human ambitions. For the strategy of mobilizing all possible resources to reach successive social goals now invites the participation of every individual and organization in both industrialized and developing nations in the task of striving for one of the great milestones in the human story – that of overcoming the worst aspects of poverty on our planet in our time. Surely the time has come to put the mass deaths of children alongside slavery, colonialism, racism, and apartheid on the shelf preserved for those things which are simply no longer acceptable to mankind. Surely the time has come to say that it is obscene to let this continue day after day, year after year, as our civilization moves into the 21st century.

ADDRESS TO THE THEOLOGICAL COLLEGE, WASHINGTON, D.C., 28 MARCH 1987

Closing the gap

We are beginning to close the vital gap between those whom you see in your daily practices and the great majority of children who will never see a physician. It has long been acknowledged that a major challenge to health professionals is to make existent techniques available to those removed from the channels of easy access. The 1980s has seen major strides in meeting this age-old challenge. Can you, in your role of leadership in the health field channel the benefits of progress and momentum now evident at the international level, into efforts in your own countries which will achieve the United Nations Year 2000 goals for child survival? Can we make the Child Survival and Development Revolution the world's most critical revolution, a revolution which will accelerate achievement of primary health care, and the goal of Health for All by the year 2000? Can we not extend the benefits of some of your most critical knowledge to the great majority of the world's children? Can we reach the unreached?

ADDRESS TO THE 15TH CONGRESS OF THE CONFEDERATION OF THE MEDICAL ASSOCIATIONS OF ASIA AND OCEANIA, BANGKOK, 2 DECEMBER 1987

The issue is leadership

There are two ways by which a country's attention to its children – and to its future – can be increased. One path is by leadership starting from the top, as when a President Betancur of Colombia ... understands that he is building a house of cards if he is building a house upon dying, sickly, disabled, stunted, unstimulated children. And so a leader takes the lead, asserts the national priority, re-allocates the national budget, and mobilizes the nation's strengths to protect and nurture the nation's children and families.

The other course is by leadership starting from below – from those who are not in power, but who are most affected or who share understanding that the city on the hill cannot shine on wasted children. This is the path taken by most of the great, progressive movements of modern history: for the abolition of slavery; for the enfranchisement of women; for the end of colonial empires; for the extension of civil rights to people of colour; and for the protection of the environment. This is the path that begins with people – like those of you involved in the Children's Defense Fund – whose voice and frustration will not be stilled. Gradually, usually ever so gradually, you are joined by more people, and then by organizations, institutions and more and more voices of authority and influence.

ADDRESS TO THE ACTION '88 NATIONAL CONFERENCE OF THE CHILDREN'S DEFENSE FUND, WASHINGTON, D.C., 9 MARCH 1988

A second arena

A second arena of unprecedented potential toward protecting children's rights exists in the prospect for passage of an international Convention on the Rights of the Child. We have heard at this session of many abuses of child rights. The Convention, which is targeted for passage by the United Nations General Assembly during the fall of 1989, represents an opportunity to establish global norms not only to discern which rights children should be assured of, but in the responsibilities of governments to protect those rights. Passage of the Convention, in itself, will not mean that children's rights will be met nor that our responsibilities toward children will be fulfilled. Rather, it will mark a milestone in the journey toward these ends – a milestone that marks, not some singular path in an isolated corner of the world, but one that maps the path of honoring child rights for all peoples. It will establish a global standard.

ADDRESS TO THE AMERICAN ACADEMY OF PEDIATRICS SYMPOSIUM ON CHILDREN AND HUMAN RIGHTS, NEW YORK, 10 MAY 1988

Toward a new world order

Crafting a new world order begins with simple visions. We in this room have those visions, I believe. We seek a world which places the individual human being at the centre of society and at the centre of the responsibilities of states. We seek a world in which each human being is assured his or her essential needs for nutrition, health and shelter; a world in which the role of the state is to foster and protect, and not abridge or neglect, the rights and dignity of each person.

We seek a world in which the human community has found a sustainable balance of its needs with the carrying capacity of the earth. And we seek a world in which nations have found a different way of inter-relating than marching across borders, carpet bombing, dueling their missiles in the sky, or starving civilians, the great majority of whom are children and their mothers.

ADDRESS TO THE 1991 INTERNATIONAL DEVELOPMENT CONFERENCE, WASHINGTON, D.C., 24 JANUARY 1991

Taking the first steps

It would be hard to have been present for those 24 hours of unprecedented history (the World Summit for Children) and say that it was a meaningless show. Few who heard those 71 leaders speak – each limited to just 3, 4 or 5 minutes – could doubt that most were learning their subject and had come to understand the fundamental insecurity of nations rooted in under-nourished, diseased, uneducated, unstimulated, neglected children. No one who participated in the preparatory process of 12 months of hard negotiation, education, persuasion and policy development – and had seen governments set in their ways yield to new appreciation of what works and why and how – could question the depth of serious engagement within governments and their policy establishment.

I suggest to you that the first step has been taken…that the World Summit for Children… was the coming together of several forces that can be, are being, and will be carried forward into a new order for the world…an order which begins with humanity's most essential, most vulnerable, and most promising citizens our children. Those converging forces include liberation from the old order of East-West confrontation and war preparations … the global flowering of democracy and resumption of history's march toward the centrality of the human person … new understandings of our capacity to ensure all people a sharing of essential resources for their basic needs … and an infectious common purpose among leaders and people (with people often in the lead, making leaders appreciate the political imperative) to get about the business of making this a decent world for all of us.

ADDRESS TO THE 1991 INTERNATIONAL DEVELOPMENT CONFERENCE,
WASHINGTON, D.C., 24 JANUARY 1991

It must be a movement for ...

To ensure that the commitments made to children in 1990 are not buried in the sand of war in 1991, or that new justifications for neglect and abuse do not again gain a foothold amid economic crises in the years to come, a worldwide movement for children – for people – is needed... a global movement akin to the movements against slavery, colonialism, environmental degradation or women's inequality... But this time, it must be a movement for, rather than a movement against, a movement allied with, and giving special dimension to, the movements for peace, environmental protection, population and other causes likely to dominate the world of the 1990s.

UNICEF ANNUAL REPORT 1991

A child like any other

What is it that transforms a child – a child like any other, filled with life, intelligence, energy and potential – into a 'street child'? There is, of course, no single answer to this question, as your discussions here this week have made abundantly clear; the circumstances vary from region to region, country to country, city to city, family to family and individual.

...the proximate causes are almost always to be found in the family – or rather, in the dysfunction and breakdown of families under stress. But the chain of events and the diverse social, economic and cultural forces coming together to push a child onto the streets go far beyond the family; more often than not, they reflect models of development that simply do not work for entire sectors of the population, an urbanization process that has shattered traditional structures, an increasingly degraded and unlivable natural environment, and inadequate or nonexistent social safety nets.

ADDRESS TO THE SECOND INTERNATIONAL CONFERENCE ON STREET
CHILDREN, RIO DE JANEIRO, 5 SEPTEMBER 1992

A few friendly provocations

…I would suggest that nobody – not the West, not the United States, nobody – 'won' the Cold War. No one emerges unscathed, unblemished or unburdened from half a century of bitter ideological warfare….

…I would argue that in our haste to proclaim the victory of the ideas of democracy and free markets – the 'End of History' – we are doing these powerful ideas a profound disservice.

…in spite of the gravity of the problems we face, I would venture to say that we have made more global human progress in the last 50 years than in the previous 2,000, to the point that three-quarters of the world's population now enjoy the basics of a life of dignity, productivity and health – progress achieved while much of the world freed itself from colonialism, and while respect for human and political rights expanded dramatically.

…the problem is not that we have tried to eradicate global poverty or even its worst symptoms, and failed; it's that no serious and concerted effort has ever been made.

…rather than requiring several generations of effort and astronomical economic resources, it is now actually possible to provide virtually every man, woman, and child on earth with adequate food, clean water, safe sanitation, primary health care, family planning, and basic education – by the end of the century and at an affordable price.

…far from taking away from much needed efforts to slow population growth, spur environmentally sustainable development, improve equality for women, and strengthen democracy, an all out assault on poverty's worst manifestations is now a precondition for resolving those burning issues of our times. It is no coincidence that countries with the highest illiteracy rates also have the highest birth rates.

Perhaps it is as the Bible says: a little child shall lead them. We need to put children first, paying special attention to the girl child; we need to give children's essential needs a 'first call' on society's resources, whether times are good or bad. If you think about it a minute, this simple principle endorsed by the world's leaders at the 1990 World Summit for Children has vast revolutionary potential. Children and women can be our Trojan horse for attacking the citadel, for undergirding democracy, dramatically slowing population growth, and for accelerating economic development.

A world of difference may separate inner city Los Angeles, Mogadiscio and the new poor of Moscow, but it is not difficult to see that many of the distinctions will surely seem irrelevant to the hungry, deprived, and frustrated in all three places. If we continue to turn our backs on the plight of the poor, or ask them to wait patiently for better days, we will reap a whirlwind for all humankind – a political, economic and environmental whirlwind that will shake even the prosperous and long-time democracies to their foundations and condemn us to a new international order of permanent conflict and instability.

If we can overcome the worst manifestations of poverty we'd be going a long way toward eradicating poverty itself, because frequent illness, malnutrition, poor growth, illiteracy, high birth rates and gender bias are not only symptoms but also some of the most fundamental causes of poverty. Accomplishing this, we could anticipate – from the recent population experiences of such diverse societies as Sri Lanka, Kerala, Costa Rica, China and the Asian NICS – a far greater reduction in the rate of population growth than most now believe possible; we'd be giving a major boost to the fragile new democracies that desperately need to provide some early measures of tangible improvement in the lives of the bottom half of their societies in order to survive; and we know from the experience of South Korea, Taiwan, Singapore and the other Asian NICS that it would accelerate economic growth. By breaking what we could call the 'inner cycle' of poverty, we would strengthen the development process' necessary assault on the many external causes of poverty, rooted in such diverse factors as geography, climate, land tenure, debt, business cycles, governance, unjust economic relations, and so on.

ADDRESS TO THE 1993 INTERNATIONAL DEVELOPMENT CONFERENCE,
WASHINGTON, D.C., 11 JANUARY 1993

A new ethos

…a new ethos…has evolved over the past half century out of the increasingly synergistic interaction between democracy and technological progress. Modern commerce, finance and transport, communications and media, on the one hand, and the environmental crisis, movements of refugees and the HIV virus, on the other, have transformed the world into a global village infused, increasingly, with democratic ideals if not consistent democratic practice.

The vast disparities in standards of living, and in levels of freedom and participation, that have existed historically, and still separate the neighbours who live side by side in this globe, are increasingly intolerable to the have-nots, and increasingly disadvantageous to the haves. As our capacity to do good has increased, it is gradually becoming unacceptable not to use that capacity, or to exclude nations, communities or individuals from the benefits of progress.

ADDRESS TO THE PEACE PRIZE FORUM, MINNESOTA, 13 FEBRUARY 1993

Thirteen million morally unconscionable deaths every year

I would argue that no features of contemporary global reality better illustrates the central human dilemma of our times than the deaths, year in and year out, of some 13 million children under the age of five. Each one of them has the same right to live, each has the same right to fulfil his or her potential, each has the same right to be loved and cared for, each has the same right to contribute to civilization, as the child of the wealthiest and most privileged of families.

For most of human history, such deaths were largely inevitable; but now we know how to prevent or cure the diarrhoea, the pneumonia, and the measles that account for most of these deaths, not only in prosperous homes but also in the world's most remote, impoverished villages, what was once tragic but largely unavoidable has become morally unconscionable – an obscenity – today. Given this welcome change – our greatly enhanced capacity to prevent child death and disability – we must ask ourselves why do so many continue to tolerate this massive needless loss of life? Should not morality march with increasing capacity?

ADDRESS TO THE EIGHTH INTERNATIONAL VATICAN CONFERENCE,
VATICAN CITY, 20 NOVEMBER 1993

We did build 'castles in the sky'

Looking back, we can sense what we have all accomplished together by having a shared vision, and by working together as developing countries...international organizations... bilateral donors... to achieve that vision of better health for children. It was a vision that seemed utopian to many in 1984, when we had our first gathering. A global recession had set in. In most countries, children were clearly the most neglected part of society. They had no legal rights – they were the property of their families. Even readily preventable and curable diseases like measles, tetanus and diarrhoea were still taking the lives of more than 10 million children annually. Only a very small proportion of the world's children were being served by the new vaccines, or benefitting from the new knowledge of how to deal with diarrhoea. Some 10 million children were dying needlessly each year – 30,000 daily – from causes for which the life-saving knowledge was there and readily available. Millions, scores of millions of children – two thirds of them girls – were out of primary school. And every-where in the early 1980s, health and education budgets were being cut under the impact of the global recession and debt crisis.

...we are setting out to do something that is beyond the powers of any of us individually. What we have been demonstrating in the last ten years is that when we work together, we really can begin to change the face of global society, the face of the world. That's both a very challenging opportunity and frankly a very great responsibility.

STATEMENT TO THE TASK FORCE FOR CHILD SURVIVAL AND DEVELOPMENT,
NEW DELHI, 4 FEBRUARY 1994

Protection issues

I would like to add my voice to that of the International Committee of the Red Cross and urge the international community to go one critical step further and adopt a total ban on the production, use, stockpiling, as well as the sale and export of anti-personnel landmines. For UNICEF, this cause has a very partic-ular force, inasmuch as the presence of landmines violates many of the fundamental provisions of the Convention on the Rights of the Child. UNICEF looks forward to being granted status in the process leading to the review conference of the Inhumane Weapons Convention, and we will participate vigorously.

...economic exploitation and sexual exploitation of children continue to demand our attention. Frankly, the trends are quite discouraging, with more and more children becoming involved in hazardous work and prostitution. UNICEF is undertaking a study to develop a better understanding of the conditions under which children are channeled into the work force and away from schooling.

Lastly, UNICEF would like to flag a complex issue for which there may not be an immediate solution, but which deserves more thoughtful attention on the part of the international community. It concerns the situation of children in countries affected by sanctions. We recognize that sanctions are a necessary tool for international action, occupying the middle ground between rhetorical resolutions and the use of armed force. Sanctions must, however, be applied in a manner in which children of poor families – the most vulnerable and the most innocent in a society – do not suffer most cruelly.

Might we not require that any proposals for sanctions include a 'child impact assessment', describing the expected impact of the proposed sanctions on children, and detailing the offsetting measures proposed to be taken?

STATEMENT DELIVERED ON MR. GRANT'S BEHALF BY MR. STEPHEN LEWIS
AT THE 50TH SESSION OF THE UNITED NATIONS COMMISSION
ON HUMAN RIGHTS, GENEVA, 8 MARCH 1994

This new construct

Today we live in an entirely different world. We expect vastly more from development because it is now seen as an integral part of a vastly greater revolution made possible by the technological advances of the last century....

In essence, thanks to this change in capacity, the world is undergoing a tectonic shift. From historical acceptance of the notion that people exist to serve their state and its elite – that under conditions of scarcity, the vast majority must labour to support the privileges of the few – we are gradually, painfully, zig-zaggingly and bravely moving toward universal acceptance of the idea that the state exists to serve people. Development, therefore, must be responsive to this new construct.

Development, if it is to be sustainable today, must not only be sustainable in the environmental sense, protecting nature and conserving scarce resources – but it also must break the grip of poverty on the bottom half or third of society and slow population growth, while sustaining democracy, human rights and people's participation in the development process.

STATEMENT AT THE 21ST WORLD CONFERENCE AT THE SOCIETY FOR
INTERNATIONAL DEVELOPMENT, MEXICO CITY, 7 APRIL 1994

This new ethic

The Convention on the Rights of the Child, with its sweeping provisions that translate children's most essential needs into rights, entered into force in 1990 after 10 long years of debate complicated by the East-West conflict. In the new atmosphere created by the end of the Cold War and the successes of the Child Survival and Development Revolution, the Convention has rapidly been embraced by more States than any other human rights treaty in history.

The Convention recognizes every child's right to develop physically, mentally and socially to his or her fullest potential, to express his or her opinions freely, and to participate in decisions affecting his or her future. This new ethic goes for girls as well as boys; it applies to children living in rural and hard-to-reach areas as well as to those living in cities and other easily accessible areas; it is as valid for children whose families and communities are poor as for those who are better off; and it should benefit children of racial, ethnic, or religious minorities as well as those from the majority or mainstream of a given society. The Convention is a Bill of Rights for all children, and a code of binding obligations for governments, communities and parents with respect to the young.

As you know, there is another category of critically important rights enshrined in the Convention – I am thinking of the provisions that protect children from exploitation and abuse. Now that the vast majority of nations have embraced the Convention, how do we judge a country's compliance in the field of child labour, for example, for which the international community has not yet adopted convenient targets and timelines? Passing and enforcing the necessary laws and regulations is obviously an essential part of what needs to happen, but eliminating such social evils is a complex undertaking that cannot be accomplished overnight in any society. But at the same time if states parties do not start moving seriously on this front, they open themselves to criticism for failing to comply with the relevant provisions of the Convention. What I am suggesting, then, is that countries where such problems are serious might consider developing national plans and timelines for compliance. Enforcement can be phased in over a realistic but not overly long timeframe.

ADDRESS AT THE MOROCCAN NATIONAL CONGRESS ON THE RIGHTS OF CHILDREN, CASABLANCA, 25 MAY 1994

A central moral imperative

It is UNICEF's belief that the time has now come to put the needs and the rights of children at the very centre of development strategy. This argument is based neither on institutional vested interest nor on sentimentality about the young; it is based on the fact that childhood is the period when minds and bodies, values and personalities are being formed and during which even temporary deprivation is capable of inflicting lifelong damage and distortion of human development.

It follows that, whether the threat be war and violence or economic marginalization, children should, as far as humanly possible, be protected from the worst mistakes and malignancies of the adult world.

For this reason, the most constant strand of UNICEF advocacy over the years has been that the vital, vulnerable years of childhood should be given a first call on societies' concerns and capacities and that this commitment should be maintained in good times and in bad. A child has only one chance to develop, and the protection of that one chance therefore demands the kind of commitment that will not be superceded by other priorities. There will always be something more immediate, there will never be anything more important.

The existence of measurable goals, deadlines and proven strategies in the areas of health, nutrition, education, water and sanitation and family planning paves the way for accelerated action for children. But due to the lack of comparable goals, deadlines and strategies in the areas of child protection and participation, we run the risk that children's rights in these equally vital areas will be neglected or relegated to a lower priority. We must not allow this to happen, especially since the Committee on the Rights of the Child has found serious and widespread problems of child abuse, exploitation and neglect in many of the countries whose reports its has reviewed.

STATEMENT TO THE THIRD COMMITTEE OF THE 49TH GENERAL ASSEMBLY
OF THE UNITED NATIONS, NEW YORK, 11 NOVEMBER 1994

'This is the true joy in life, the being used for a purpose recognised by yourself as a mighty one. I am of the opinion that my life belongs to the whole community and as long as I live it is my privilege to do for it whatever I can. Life is no brief candle to me. It is a sort of splendid torch which I have got hold of for the moment, and I want to make it burn as brightly as possible before handing it on to future generations.'

JIM GRANT'S FAVOURITE QUOTATION FROM GEORGE BERNARD SHAW, WITH WHICH HE ENDED HIS LAST STATE OF THE WORLD'S CHILDREN REPORT.